SMART JOCKS

10 LESSONS ALONG OUR JOURNEY TO RAISE

#1 DRAFT PICKS ON AND OFF THE COURT

Dear Jordan,

The Sky is the limit
Just follow the blueprint!

Dr. Andrea
Jeffress

Car Accou?

1 h step is the limit-

just follow the blueprint.

Business
Coffee?

SMART JOCKS

10 Lessons Along Our Journey to Raise
#1 Draft Picks On and Off the Court

Drs. Andrea & William Jeffress

With Foreword by

Mike Gallagher

Freelance Multi-Media Sports Journalist and Producer

for Jet TV 24 ABC/FOX 66, ESPN, and NFL Films

SMART JOCKS  PUBLISHING

ERIE

SMART JOCKS

10 LESSONS ALONG OUR JOURNEY TO RAISE #1 DRAFT PICKS ON AND OFF THE COURT

SMART JOCKS Publishing
A division of SMART JOCKS, LLC
P.O. Box 9635, Erie, PA 16505

Special discounts are available for bulk quantity purchases by teams, schools, community centers, gyms or athletic facilities, churches, book clubs, associations, prisons, or other special interest groups. For information about bulk purchases, the SMART JOCKS Career and College Readiness Portal or the Workbook and Planner, please visit the website at www.smartjocks.com and contact us at info@smartjocks.com.

Cover Art Illustration by Feliberto Mendez, Jr.
Cover Design by Paul Adamaszek, Faulkner's Screen Printing

Library of Congress Cataloging-in-Publication Data:
International Standard Book Number: 978-1-732-2011-1-8
Library of Congress Control Number: 2018908917

1 2 3 4 5 6 7 8 9 10

Printed in the United States of America

Just in time for back to school!

The SMART JOCKS Tool Kit

TABLE OF CONTENTS

INVICTUS

Out of the night that covers me,
Black as the Pit from pole to pole,
I thank whatever gods may be
For my unconquerable soul.

In the fell clutch of circumstance
I have not winced nor cried aloud.
Under the bludgeonings of chance
My head is bloody, but unbowed.

Beyond this place of wrath and tears
Looms but the Horror of the shade,
And yet the menace of the years
Finds, and shall find, me unafraid8

It matters not how strait the gate,
How charged with punishments the scroll.
I am the master of my fate:
I am the captain of my soul.

by WILLIAM ERNEST HENLEY

DEDICATION

This book is dedicated...

To the five beautiful children we raised, Adrianna, Jasmine and William, and our niece and nephew, Juanita, and Terrance, who we pray are inspired everyday by our example to use the gifts God blessed them with and strive for excellence in every aspect of their lives;

To our loving Mothers, Rosalind Toulson and Dorothy Jeffress, who nurtured us, empowered us, and sacrificed so much so that we could reach our full potential.

To a loving Father George Toulson, Sr., who lost his battle to cancer, but never stopped fighting to live the life of a transformed man saved by God.

To a loving sister, Rosalie Diane Jeffress, who was taken from us too soon, but helped plant the competitive seeds in her brother's life to pursue athletics and education.

To our Brothers and Sisters, Demetria, Gebrette, George and Charles for their loving support in every possible way.

To our nieces and nephews, Quentin, Trevor, Bryant, Austin, Brooklyn, and Harrison, and God Children Janelle, Chase, Darius and Cyrus whose futures are bright and full of strength to fight.

To our extended family in Connecticut, New York, New Jersey, Delaware, California, Texas, and Pennsylvania. Our favorite Aunts Queen, Vera, and Aunt Delores- "Bootsy"- and all her awesome sons, our cousins, and their wives, who never stop rooting for us.

To the powerful prayer warriors and seers Metashar, Kim, Amber, Chandra, Pam, Nicole, and Kelly. Our God Mothers, Sharon Alexander, Janice McElrath and our children's' Godfather, Albert Mattie; Our children's' Godmothers, Metashar Dillon and Tammy Lamb Manning, MD.

To all the parents and family members of student-athletes who try to be supportive and be present in their child's life to provide even the simplest advantage needed to succeed;

The dedicated coaches and mentors who work tirelessly to be a steady guide and resource for their players and their teams to propel them to greatness; To Metashar for pushing like no other and being an example of faith and women in entrepreneurship.

And finally, to the SMART JOCKS all over the world who embrace the process and challenge themselves to be the best they can be on and off the court.

This book is dedicated to all of you who dare to dream the impossible dream.

GRATITUDES:
"Thank You for The Ride"

Since there are no rules when it comes to saying thank you, we want to take you on a long joy ride of gratitude...

We are grateful for so much support in our lives and for support during this challenging process.

First, we are grateful for the grace, blessings and favors that God has shown upon our lives and the lives of our children - Adrianna, Jasmine, William Jr. and nephew, Terrance, and niece, Juanita, during this project and labor of love for all their help and support with millennial advice, administrative and tech support, copy editing, writing contributions and research. It was a family affair, and you are all angels in our lives.

God really blessed us when he gave us our mothers, Rosalind and Dorothy. They are a true testament to God's grace and mercy, strength and wisdom. Thank you for instilling in us a great work ethic and loving us unconditionally. We appreciate your supporting us without question through the good, the bad and the ugly. You are, by far, our first and best coaches and the best groupies a son and daughter could ever have.

To our Fathers, both gone now, George Sr. and William Cyrus. We are in sincere gratitude for the gift of life. Especially, we want to thank George Sr. for his inspiration of independence through entrepreneurship and his example of marriage ministry and faith. He wrote a marriage ministry book called, "Our Marriage, Our

Marriage" with his second wife, Bertha Toulson, aka Mom Bee, just before he died. Although he lost his fight to cancer, he never gave up fighting to live his life as a transformed man saved by God. Thanks Mom Bee for being there to help God do a mighty work in him.

We also have so much gratefulness for our Grandparents: Pop-Pop Charles Earl, Grandma Dot, Grandma Louise and Mimi who taught us the value of land, hard work and helped to raise us to love God and fear no one. Many thanks to Mrs. Betty Dixon and the Dixon family, the Coughlin Family, the Morris Family, the Thomas Family, The Paul Family, The Hilliard Family, The Williams Family, and the Grace Family for being our Erie extended family when it was needed most.

To our brothers and sisters - Demetria, Gebrette, George and Charles, who are all examples of what family should be - awesome help spirits and treasured gifts. Thank you for your faith and investing in us. We love you guys so much; To our sisters and from another mister, Metashar, Wesley, Tammy, Karen, Annette, and Marva. Thanks for your friendship during the best and the toughest times.

A very special thanks to:

Our publishing consultant, Desiree Lee – creator and founder of the #1 Self-Publishing company, Authors in Business. Thank you for sharing your gift with the world and inspiring us to finish. You have nurtured the #AIBNation into a great movement and supportive self-publishing community. #WeMoveAsOne.

We are also extremely grateful to Mr. M.H. Noman and Mr. Cole Gordon (-aka- Mr. Fancy) for their calm patience, laser-like efficiency, skillful technical expertise, and attention to detail in the manuscript preparation and formatting of the books. They made one of the hardest parts of self-publishing a book feel like a breeze.

Thank you to Mike Gallagher, our friend and media veteran guru, who wrote the foreword to the book and has been a driving force behind the media and marketing to get us where we are today. We cannot thank him enough for all he has done.

Thank you to Feliberto "Bio" Mendez, Jr., a talented artist, illustrator and musician, for his amazing commissioned cover artwork through his business "Art by Feliberto" and to Paul Adamaszek of Faulkner's Screen Printing for his expert graphics design work for the cover design and print merchandising assistance. We have never met two gentlemen with so much skill and patience!

Andrea - thanks to all the coaches and teachers at Sanford school and Simon's Rock of Bard College for giving me the tools to be successful in medicine and business. All those years of free writing are paying off. And thank you to my classmate Veronica for reviewing one of my essays, sending out her blog consistently – the Tiny Letter – which is always encouraging me that I could do it.

Bill -Thank you to all the teachers and coaches within Long Branch, NJ Public Schools for instilling a love in education and athletics that drives me today; Especially, Coach Odom and his wife Mrs. O, and his college basketball Coach Grove and his wife, Mrs. Grove, who went beyond the call of duty to be like father figures, mentors and friends.

Thanks to our partners and co-workers at OB/GYN Associates and Mercyhurst University for promoting a business and family culture to allow working parents to prioritize their families in a such a vital way. Thanks for always giving back to the community and supporting our civic endeavors.

A special thank you to our Entrepreneurship Family – Our GV and Next Level Leadership Families, the Future Trends International China and USA A-Team, our RainEater Wiper Blade Family (voted number one by consumers!), our Zenedge Energy Drink Family. We have achieved much success because of your unwavering support.

Thanks for our community support team and coaching family for all the network support to build a team we can be proud of in order to help our kids become successful - especially their primary Coaches - Head Tennis Pro Ric Harden, Jerry Simon, John Cavanaugh, Jamie Soboleski, Kevin O'Connor, Cliff Beck, Bill Firch, Justin Izbicki, Jason Keim; Dr. Delullo for expert medical treatment, Paul Enders and his awesome athletic training staff for injury rehab, prevention and treatment, Coach Paul Esser and Jeff "Lumpy" Gibbons strength and conditioning coaches, you have sown a seed into our lives that is invaluable.

Thanks to our awesome teachers and local school administrators who go above and beyond the call of duty - Millcreek Superintendent Bill Hall, Athletic Director Mark Becker & athletic office staff, McDowell High School Principal Mr. Brian Fuller, Asst. Principals, Mrs. Kimberly Damcott and Mr. Justin Izbicki, and McDowell Intermediate High School Principal, Dr. John Cavanaugh, school counselors Mrs. Rys and Mr. Boyd. Thank you for your tremendous dedication and unwavering support to pursue excellence in education and sport and emotional well-being. Much gratitude again to Coach Ric and to the Westwood Tennis and Racket Center Community hitting partners like owner Tom Pakulski, Jeet Saberwaal, and the many other tennis coaches Mio, Kim, Faiga, Ryan, Keith and community members-Dennis, Ravi, Brian, Kevin, Mark, Eddie, Matt, Rahul, Mike, Landon, Greg and the amazing front desk staff, Leslie, Ann Marie, Michelle, and Laura who made Westwood a great place to train.

Thanks to our travel basketball family - John Cavanaugh and the Baller parents and teammates; Sonny Johnson, Demetrius "Meechie" Johnson, Juby Johnson; Mike Pisano, Principle of Erie High School, coach, father of Vincent Pisano and husband to Michele Pisano for all the trips as parents and teammates we made around the country and up and down the road to train our kids; Mike Jones of Game Speed Basketball Training for the one on one work outs; thanks to Coach Coverdale and Coach Terrell at We Are One and Team Durant: Kevin Durant and his father Wayne Pratt, Roderick, Kingston, Coach Oz, Bobo, Burke, Avery, Doc, and Janelle Murphy – for all the support to grow and develop to chase that dream of being a top draft pick.

Finally, we want to thank each other for hanging in there with one another. Marriage isn't always glamorous or easy; it is never perfect, but we are perfect for each other. Through the good and bad times, we have found a way to lift one another up. We continue to make it through the rough patches to brighter days by exercising faith, patience, communication, a willingness to love despite faults, and forgiveness.

Our philosophy is marriage is like a car - a finely tuned, well-oiled machine, relying on important safety features and needing the drivers and passengers to assume different roles when needed. Of course, there's a steering wheel. He's driving, but and when he gets tired of steering and leading, especially at night (lol), we switch drivers. Where one person is the set of windshield wipers, clearing up and focusing our vision, the other is the rearview mirror and backup camera, protecting the other's back. Where one is the gas, the other person is the brakes. A car can't function without both. So we are thankful for the acceleration - the encouraging nudge, the not so subtle kick in the pants, or that great big push to finish what you've started. In turn, we commit to remain open and receptive to the one who speaks up to say, "proceed with caution", the one pushing on the pedal to come to a gentle slow down or a life-saving hard stop. We need both from time to time when we need inspiration to keep going or to be our protector when we get reckless and need redirection. We miss our new car days and recognize that sometimes an older car needs to be put in service. We never like the service bill, but whatever the cost, we try to keep the engine running smoothly. We feel blessed to be still riding strong in our sweet, semi-vintage 1995 coupe (well honestly, more like a 1995 minivan), and for that we are eternally grateful.

Thank you for the ride...

SHORT STORY:
by Andrea Jeffress, MD

"Draft Day"

30 years ago, after taking a long car ride on a bitter cold, winter evening, I was turned away from Trump Plaza Hotel and Casino by a miraculous act of divine intervention.

It was New Year's Eve, December 31st, 1988. I was home from college on Christmas break. My sister, Demetria, had turned 21 and was finally "legal", and she wanted to go to Atlantic City to celebrate. She began to scheme a plan because my Mom would likely not let her go alone. Although I was only 18 and she was 21, I had left home for college when I was 14 so I was already a junior in college at Simon's Rock of Bard College. I was the super-brainy, level-headed one. My mother would never consent for her to go alone with other friends without me.

All day Demetria harassed me while I was studying. Yes, I was studying for my MCATs that were coming up in the spring during the Christmas break. I finally gave in to end the incessant beating on my bedroom door, which she eventually knocked off the hinges – yes this really happened – but I only agreed to go after striking a deal with my sister. The deal was, if she agreed to leave me alone for the whole rest of the Christmas break so that I could study for my MCATs in the spring, I would go with her and her friends to Atlantic City celebrate her milestone. And our Mom would say yes.

Her plan was coming together nicely. There was only one problem – I had nothing suitable to wear. However, that little issue would not thwart my sister's master plan to get my mother's permission to go on her first "legal" road trip. My one-woman glam squad, she began to rummage through my suitcase, flinging clothes everywhere about the room. Finally, after her tornado fashion frenzy, she had assembled my very best outfit option for my first New Year's Eve: plain, black khakis and a long sleeved, white, button-up polyester blouse, accessorized with a costume jewelry gold broach at the nape of my neck. She topped it off with a mustard sweater that had a button missing. I swept my hair up into a high crown style with the front crimped with an electric crimping iron and made one giant French braid down the middle. With that, I was ready for my first New Year's Eve.

Before we could jump onto the ramp for the New Jersey Turnpike, my sister made an abrupt stop at "Farmers Market", the outdoor flea market in the center of New Castle, Delaware. My first thought was "Good – I'm so hungry. We can pick up some fruit for the road". But instead, we got out of the car and made our way to this shady, outdoor tent covered on all sides with dirty white flaps. We lifted up the entry door flap and walked inside. Naïve me, I did not realize we were there to order a fake ID. You see – even though I was a junior in college – I did not know how to drive or have my license yet.

I remember it being very dim and extremely smoky inside the tent, enough to make your throat tickle a little. Behind the makeshift counter, there was a crotchety, old, white man who was sitting down a dusty desk. He began typing as he took my sister's order. "What's her name? What's her address? How old is she? What year was she born?" We argued over the math for the birthdate to make me 21. I won that argument.

We walked out of the clandestine tent and back into the bright chill of the New Year's Eve night with the fakest ID ever created on the face of the earth. It was literally a cheap, plastic, laminated card with my name, address, age and DOB typed on it. So, now armed with my "certified" Farmers' Market ID, we hit the road.

Unfortunately, but fortunately, once we arrived at the Trump Plaza Hotel and Casino, I was turned away from the door because this horrible attempt at a legitimate ID did not pass. My sister's friends were so angry. They fussed and cussed, "We told you not to bring her!" - along with some other choice words. So, we hopped back into the car and drove around Atlantic City until they found a decent enough place to dump me so that they could return to Trump Casino. The club we stumbled upon was called Fridaze. The driver pulled up to the curb and dropped me off on the sidewalk. They told me they'd be back to get me at 4 am.

Nervously, I made my way to the end of the line to get in, which wrapped around the outside of the building with women that all looked like Diana Ross with all their glitz and glam. When I finally reached the door dressed in my best college threads with no makeup and no hair do, I almost did not get in again with my Farmers Market ID. But the bouncer took pity on me after I began to cry real crocodile years, telling him the story of how my sister left me. So, with no cover money and no ID, he let me in and told me to stand next to him at the door and don't move. And so, I stood there on a wall next just inside the doorway next to the bouncer for hours! Then the ball dropped – 10, 9, 8, 7…3, 2, 1! The crowd shouted, "Happy

New Year!" Although I was alone, tired, hungry, and thirsty, I, too, shouted out to the anonymous crowd, "Happy New Year!"

Then something miraculous happened. Shortly after the countdown to midnight, my husband, a 6'6" handsome and tall drink of water, walked up to me and asked me to dance! I reluctantly looked over to the bouncer to ask for permission with pleading eyes only. He rolled his own eyes in his head and nodded yes. After standing obediently just inside the door for hours, I could finally move.

We exchanged pleasantries and names and then we danced and laughed the night away. Then suddenly, out of nowhere, we had one deep, magnetic kiss. Everything in me tingled. I was pretty much sold on him right then and there.

After we danced, he asked few questions, but not the usual pick-up lines. No. This first question he asked me caught me way off guard. Bill asked, "What are your goals and objectives?" I was so stunned and frozen for a flash second. Wait - what kind of pick up line was this? Whatever happened to getting to know each other with questions like "What's your favorite color?" or "What's your zodiac sign?". I snapped out of it and chirped back quickly, "I'm going to be a doctor. What are you going to be?" He replied, "I'm getting my master's degree in business now, I'm going to be a basketball coach, and I want to get my doctorate someday, too." He then proceeded to tell me he would not marry a woman for five years until he could get to really know her. And I quickly told him no one wanted to marry him, and any way, I promised my mother that I would finish college and medical school before I would ever consider marrying someone. But I was intrigued. Truthfully, I had never met a guy who looked like him and who had goals like me. I was smitten…from the start.

The rest is history. After dating for 6 years (he stayed true to his word, and I ended up asking him to hurry up and marry me – lol), twenty-three years of marriage and 3 amazing children later, I am thankful for being turned away from Trump Hotel and Casino that night. What a twist of fate that I would meet my future husband, Bill, who became my amazing New Year's blessing in 1989. That was the day I got drafted.

I once asked him what he saw in me that night – why me? He said, "Of all the women in the club with sequin gowns, 5-inch heels, big hair weave, fake eye lashes, fingernails, and you name whatever else they wore, you were the realest person in the room.

Though life has never been as perfect as that special "Draft Day", I am so very grateful that God sent me you. You are our rock. I want to thank you from the bottom of my heart for being the most supportive husband, father, business partner, coach and super fan in our lives. I feel especially blessed that you allow us so much room to grow and the freedom to pursue our many passions wherever they take us in the world. You are truly special and one of a kind. I love you, and I am so proud I was your number one draft pick.

FOREWORD

I am extremely honored to write this foreword.

Initially, I thought I should deliver this message about my unique relationship to the authors and the subject from the perspective of a seasoned, 30-year media veteran. As a former TV sports news anchor and ESPN and NFL freelance contributor and producer who has been nominated for two Emmys, I have covered professional and amateur sports across the United States. I have had the honor to film and report on Dan Marino and the Miami Dolphins, the Cleveland Browns, the Pittsburgh Steelers, Chris Paul and the Los Angeles Clippers, and LeBron James and Cleveland Cavaliers. On an amateur level, I have covered universities and high schools, such as James Conner and the University of Pittsburgh Panthers, Edinboro University, Gannon University, Mercyhurst University, Slippery Rock University, Allegheny College, Indiana University of Pennsylvania, McDowell, Cathedral Prep, Villa, Mercyhurst Prep, Erie High, Girard, Harbor Creek, Corry, Northwestern, Fort LeBoeuf, General McLane, Grove City, Sharon, Kennedy Catholic, and so many others. That makes me somewhat of an expert in amateur and professional sports. However, knowing what went in to the publication of "SMART JOCKS", I realized it would be much more appropriate for me to share my testimony on a personal level.

As a sports-media specialist with millions of views and followers on Facebook, I could have never imagined 18 years ago what my relationship would be like with this family who had two beautiful, little daughters and a niece and a nephew when they moved into the house behind me. The husband, Bill, came over to introduce himself, saying the only reason he bought the house on the huge corner lot was because in a few years he was going to have a son, and he wanted to know if they would be welcome to shoot on my hoop. We became friendly neighbors, sharing adjoining backyards with myself, my wife Lisa, and our 5 children. His wife, Dr. Jeffress, who quickly established a reputation as one of the best new doctors in our Erie community, somehow happened to be the obstetrician on call at the hospital the night my 6th child, Jack, was born. Two years later, their son William was born, and just as his father spoke it, he took his first basketball shot on my hoop in my backyard when he was only two years old.

One stormy night, I was in my backyard photographing an ominous storm looming in the distance when I captured a dramatic frame of a lightning bolt that lit up the night sky, illuminating the Jeffress home. Years later, when William would become the prodigy of our Erie and statewide Pennsylvania basketball community, I would recall that moment and record it for my Vimeo account. I knew that night there was something special in the air and in the incredible destiny we shared.

That destiny is manifesting now. They say it takes a village to raise a child. I learned firsthand that the people in that village are instrumental in how a child develops. Now when you add in what it takes to raise an athlete and a student, the role of this village rises to a whole new level. Yes, I did spend thirty years covering professional and high school athletes as they strived for success both on and off the field, but my personal, unique experience with Dr. Andrea Jeffress and Dr. William Jeffress relates directly to my own six children and being a single father to them after losing their mother to brain cancer a few years ago.

Each one of my children has played a sport at some level. Each and every step of the way the Jeffresses were there when my kids needed more than just a single father. My youngest son, Jack, is now an up and coming high school basketball player, hoping to develop well enough to play basketball at the collegiate level while earning a degree. In his development, he was fortunate that the Jeffresses were there to lend guidance to him as he worked on the court and did what he could to make his academic status worthy of consideration from collegiate coaches.

Unlike the Jeffress family, we got into the game late and spent the good part of Jack's high school career getting to a point where coaches would notice his play and believe in his potential to play college basketball. Now we have no false hope of him ever being one of those elite players that makes it to the NBA; but with guidance from the Jeffress family, we have come to realize that, with the proper work ethic, determination, and the willingness to set priorities, my son can have a chance to be that number one draft pick in all aspects of his life. They have counseled with him, advocated for him, and pushed him to reach his full potential, and Jack has responded as only Jack can - with spirit, with grit, and a get-under-your-skin, never-give-up attitude. With work on leadership and emotional intelligence, Jack has learned to channel his aggression and make smart plays on and off the floor. With their no nonsense and practical approach, they have become a consistent sounding board in his personal development and a key part of our team and our growing village.

In the same fashion, "SMART JOCKS" lays the foundation for being successful when it comes to developing a young student-athlete. "SMART JOCKS" are those kids who are raised in a way that puts them at the head of the class. We all want our kids to be that kid. In this day in age, no matter what the talent level, it is critical to put emphasis on an athlete's life outside of the game. "SMART JOCKS" is a great read that provides the blueprint to success. This book does more than just give you a few tips; it walks you through those life lessons that are essential to raising a number one draft pick on and off the court.

The one thing I can guarantee you is that the authors of this book put their heart and soul into raising their own number one draft picks. Now they are ready to share all they have learned along their journey. While there may be many trials and tribulations involved with raising a top-notch student-athlete, "SMART JOCKS" gives you the tools to turn an uphill challenge into an amazing voyage, full of lifelong special moments that you and your family will cherish for generations to come.

Mike Gallagher

Multi-Media Sports Journalist

Jet TV 24 ABC/FOX 66 - Erie

ESPN, Freelance Journalist and Producer

NFL Films, Freelance Journalist and Producer

PREFACE

Smart Jocks are special athletes that defy all stereotypes. They possess a strong, physical, competitive nature and yet are blessed with an assertive, introspective and cerebral gift. They are talented children who demonstrate both a genius-level athletic prowess and an admirable academic brilliance. Nowhere in this description does it say they are perfect, but they are perfect examples of the new standard of cool - kids who make it the norm to be stars in the classrooms and phenoms in sports.

Smart Jocks are the kids everyone wants to draft first at recess. As they grow older, they become the adolescents and young adults that high schools, colleges, graduate schools, recruiters, advertisers, companies, businesses, boards, and professional teams want to draft in the first round to their team. They are the geese that lay the golden eggs, the legacies that last a thousand years.

The truth is we all dream that person is our child - a promise that God gave. And we, the authors, were no exception.

As parents, both former athletes ourselves, we have always dreamed of harnessing the power of athletics and academics to catapult our family to an elite level life. Each one of our children has maintained a 3.8 to 4.0 GPA while playing pivotal team roles and winning accolades along the way, such as Team Captain, Most Spirited Player, All-State Honors, Trojan Female Athlete of the Year, 2018 MaxPreps High School Boys' Basketball Freshman All-American Team, and ESPN Boys' Basketball Top 10.

For us, sports and good grades were our way up and out of poverty - a way to build wealth for a new generation. So, we set out to continue building upon our family's legacy the best way we knew how - using a ball and a book.

The number one question we faced was a simple one, but it did not appear to have a simple answer. Why have some student-athletes been successful in reaching some of their goals, but not others? Is it God-given talent or environment or a combination of both? If you are not sure, you are not alone. This question is being asked by a host of folks from parents to coaches, teachers, administrators, recruiters, agents, sports professionals, and student-athletes themselves. We believe that God blesses you the talent; however, it's up to us to use that talent to the best of our ability using our faith to drive our dreams, self-discipline, hard work and perseverance to manifest all the gifts that God has bestowed upon us.

So, what should we do to make the most of our special gifts?

For the reader who is a parent, family member, mentor or coach, the main goal of the book is to provide some basic tips and principles of goal setting, planning, strategy, management, leadership, decision making, financial literacy, teamwork, recruitment, and mental preparation. It is beneficial for the student athlete to read as well because he or she can see that there is a reason for everything - a method to the madness. Have you heard the old adage, "It takes a village to raise a child"? Well, in the sports world, we have concluded, "It takes a team to raise a SMART JOCK." The student athletes that are most successful have likely had someone on their team that has given time and attention to master some aspect of these areas to develop their player into a brilliant and fierce competitor.

For the student reader, if you want to be a number one draft pick in the classroom, in your sporting venue, or in your future career (which might not even be professional sports), then you must prepare early for this journey. This book is also designed to help you use self-assessment, athletic training, academic/study skills, and mental skills to take your God-given gifts to the next level by working on your personal development. If you are not going to go pro in sports, you can go pro in something else in life with a successful career in the classroom, on the court, on the field, on the job, in business or entrepreneurship, and in life.

We are living in a time where some people believe everybody deserves a trophy; however, we all know there are limited seats within the classroom, limited spots on a team, and limited opportunities for careers. Research on achievement suggests that successful people reach their personal and professional goals not simply because of who they are, but more often because of what they do; hence the saying "hard work beats talent every time". In today's society, academic and athletic success is based on our preparation. Therefore, if we would like our children to use their blessings and talents to be great, we must prepare them early to compete on all levels.

However, this journey to greatness, though team oriented, has to be a shared vision, not just the dream or delusion of the parent. There are different levels in which your child may have opportunities to compete. The sooner you and your child decide the level you both agree on where they should be, the better. There are different levels of self-discipline that are required to foster greater success. The sooner you and your child decide the level of commitment you both agree upon, the better. As parents, mentors, and coaches, we need to be wary of and avoid the pitfall of the transference of our goals onto our kids. At some point, being a number one draft pick has to be their goal, not ours. They must have the will to win and the heart to pursue their goals. The dream ultimately starts and ends with them. As the famed coach, Vince Lombardi, once said:

"The difference between a successful person and others is not a lack of strength, not a lack of knowledge, but rather a lack of will."

With that said, this book is our humble attempt to share with you many lessons that may help you along on your journey to raising #1 draft picks, focusing on setting a foundation that will help students and their support system achieve success along their journey. Everyone's path and situation is different - we are married, but some may be single; we have modest means, whereas some family financial situations may range from poverty to ultra-wealthy; some will have minimal coaching resources and others have access to the best coaching available. It would be narrow minded to think that there is just one way to do things - there never is. These are just a few ideas and concepts that may be helpful along the way. Feel free to evaluate your own circumstances and apply the practical knowledge in an ethical and professional manner to prepare your kids to compete in a competitive society and get your student-athlete across the finish line.

Whatever you do, commit to doing it well. Have faith and dream big. Be in it to win it. Don't just participate, have a mindset to dominate. It's not just about hard work, it's about smart work. Learn to weather life's hard knocks and be a SMART JOCK.

Lesson 1

Dream Big, Dream in Stereo

*"You don't get in life what you want,
you get in life what you believe."*

- Oprah Winfrey

Dream the Dream

The most beautiful part of life is permission to dream. When Bill and I met in Atlantic City, while I was in college and he was in graduate school, we bonded over what seemed to be a simple but loud dream. He said he wanted to have five children because he dreamed of having a basketball team. I was 18, naive, and so much in love that I quickly nodded yes to what would be surely five noisy and rowdy kids without a moment's thought.

It was wonderful that we both shared a love and a passion of sports despite our different paths in life. He had been a Green-Wave All-Star at Long Branch High School in New Jersey on the Jersey shore under the beloved tutelage of Coach Bentley "O" Odom. Then he was recruited on a full basketball scholarship to the University of New Haven where he was nicknamed "Dollar Bill" because his shot was "money in the bank". He scored over 1000 points in both high school and college and was inducted into Athletic Hall of Fames at each institution. Following college, he was drafted to the semi-pro league by the New Haven Skyhawks, but in a turn of bad fortune, as he and his peers were getting called up to the pros for teams like the Phoenix Suns, he injured his back and had to retire.

After some thought about life after basketball, he decided to enroll in graduate school and became a graduate assistant coach for the UNH Men's Basketball team which was led by his amazing coach and mentor, Stewart "Stu" Grove. He earned his Master's in Business Administration while coaching and then went on to forge a career in Sport Business Management and higher education. He became an athletic director and coach at the college level at Post University, Senior Assistant Athletic Director at Yale University, and Director of College Life for Gateway Community College. Currently, he teaches Sport Business Management at Mercyhurst University.

My journey in sports was a very different one. In terms of talent, I was an average, but passionate, all-around athlete. The prestigious high school I attended was called Sanford School, 45 minutes outside of the inner-city limits of Wilmington, Delaware where I grew up. I failed the entrance exam initially, and then my mother tutored me over the summer. I retook the entrance exam again and passed. It was a long commute every day but getting into Sanford School was one of the best things that ever happened to me.One of the things that made the school unique was that Sanford was so small that it was mandatory for all students to play a sport every season just to field school teams. As a young black girl from "the hood" - lol - this was very foreign to me. But without a choice, I learned to play field hockey and volleyball in the fall, basketball in the winter, and lacrosse and track in the spring - except there was one problem. I was slow as molasses, and everyone knew it. However, what I lacked in speed and athleticism, I made up with smarts and grit. Although I was not the star of any of the teams I played on, I was intelligent, a quick learner, a leader, and a fierce competitor. I learned the value of being assertive and aggressive to get the win. The long commute and always having to stay after school for sporting activities forced me to develop physical stamina, a focused self-discipline, critical time-management skills, a strong resilience, and quiet tenacity that would sneak up on you before you ever knew it. Playing sports year-round in high school would be my greatest asset in college and medical school. I was never daunted and never backed down from a challenge.

When my husband mentioned his dream of a basketball team, I guess five kids seemed no different of a challenge. There was only one stipulation that I requested before I would agree and that was "equal opportunity". I demanded that if I had girls, he would treat them the same way he would treat my boys. The way I see it, participation in sports is great for girls because it builds strong women - and strong women build strong nations. He agreed. So, it was settled. We dreamed the dream and chose to live a shared vision and mission.

A Dream Deferred

Early in our marriage, during medical school and residency, we faced a family crisis. We learned that Bill's sister, Rosalie, had an addiction to drugs. Her lifestyle brought on numerous health problems and ultimately took her life. We were all heart broken. To avoid the possible perils of the social service system, we became guardians of our nephew and niece, Terrance and Juanita, who were very special to us. With the help of my mother who kept them for two years and Bill's mother, Dorothy, who helped to support them, the kids blossomed into great adolescents. Then God blessed us with two of our own beautiful girls - Adrianna and Jasmine. Terrance and Juanita were a God-send during my training because they were more like siblings to our kids than cousins; they helped us with the little ones so much.

However, with a growing family, there were always challenges. Suddenly, a light bulb went off in my head. Well maybe it was not a light bulb - perhaps it was more like a panic siren. Like a ton of bricks, it hit me that this labor of love was going to be a tough assignment. Caring for four kids and being working parents as a full-time OB/GYN physician and an athletic and education business administrator, I began to ask myself in my head, "What were you thinking? You had to be insane to agree to a basketball team."

After I finished medical school and residency training at Yale, I was recruited to move to Erie, Pennsylvania for a fantastic job offer with an awesome group called OB/GYN Associates of Erie. Ironically, the move happened the same year of the record snowfall when Erie was one of the top three cities in the United States for snow. Every day, it was a winter wonderland, and the snow reached as high as the mailboxes. I thought to myself, "Dear God, what have I done?" However, Juanita never missed one day of high school for inclement weather because the schools never closed. Nothing ever shut down - not the mall, not the doctor's office, not the hospital, not the city! Nothing! We eventually adjusted. In 2018, we set a record with 7 feet of snow over the course of a few days. The snow became what we are known for, our badge of honor.

After settling in Erie, we began talking about the dream again - you know, the "basketball team" - only I had a change of heart. We had two girls and our niece and nephew. Bill was so disappointed like I pulled a bait and switch and punched him in the gut. "No. That was not the deal", he said passionately (read angrily). I told him when I agreed to the "deal", I was 18 and had no idea what it meant to be a working parent. Suddenly, I recognized that the job our own parents did to raise us was a huge accomplishment - even more amazing was that a good bit of that time raising us was done as single mothers.

Even with this reasoning, Bill was still intent on holding my feet to the fire. So, I agreed to try one more time. In keeping with the sports theme that he so cherished, I told him, "This is like baseball - three strikes, buddy, and you're out!" If he did not get a boy this time, he was out of luck! That year his present was a Christmas card with glossy sonogram picture inside - unmistakably endowed as a baby boy - which read, "Merry Christmas - This is all you're getting!" William Jr. was born in Erie a months later.

Be Patient While Your Dreams Manifest

Fast-forward several years later - minus the basketball team - and here we were both working full-time, caring for our five kids, volunteering in community work, and living in a place where none of our family resided. Yet, no matter the obstacles, we had a dream, a shared vision and mission, that our kids would be immersed in a life of sports because we both had received so many benefits from sports being a part of our lives.

Terrance played basketball, track/cross-country, baseball, and football; Juanita played basketball and soccer; Adrianna played basketball and switched to tennis; Jasmine played basketball, track, and then fell in love with volleyball; and William played tennis and volleyball for a hot minute, but eventually concentrated on a single sport - of course - basketball (this one would never get away).

We cannot ever recall ever giving any of the kids much choice as to whether to play or not play sports. We became very good at balancing the idea of fun-loving participation with just enough motivational push to achieve the desired result - a well-rounded student-athlete poised for success on and off the court.

Much of their success happened because we showed interest in their activities and loved them. Another a critical piece of our success was that each child was the beneficiary of our on-the-job training with the previous child. We learned through our experiences, triumphs and tribulations with each subsequent child. As parents, the learning curve of each sport system was steep, but we got the hang of it.

I would say our only regrets are that we let Terrance quit football and Jasmine quit tennis when we should have pushed each of them to continue to use their God-given talent and gifts. We could have also shown Adrianna more support in tennis from a family perspective.

That was how our dream manifested - with patience and perseverance and a little trial and error – getting better and better at system with age and each subsequent child. Although we did not have our own basketball team, what mattered most was that each child claimed their own happiness - and that was priceless. You too will have to figure out what your dream is and let destiny patiently unfold.

> *"The biggest break is the one you will give yourself by choosing to believe in your vision, in what you love, and in the gifts, you have to offer the world." – Leslie Odom, Jr.*

Let Your Why Guide Your Dream

Once there is a dream in mind, you must realize that each family's path for participation and success in sports will be unique. Everyone's rationale and motivation for putting their kids in sports will be different. The most important thing is to figure out your "Why" and define your purpose. You must then ask yourself the question, "What do I want sports to do for my family?"

Are you using sports to do any of the following?

- Build character
- Promote a healthy lifestyle
- Manage illness such as fighting diabetes or childhood obesity
- Develop leadership skills
- Earn a discounted education
- Find a way up and out of poverty to wealth and prosperity
- Accolades and fame

Or, all of the above?

In summary, give yourself permission to dream. Take the limits off your mind and set about creating a plan to capture the desires of your heart and wildest imagination. Figure out your "Why" and your purpose, so that you can set goals for your level participation, commitment and training. Recognize that no dream of yours or your child's is too small or too big, and it is worthy to be said out loud so that it can be fulfilled on the most practical or grandest of scales.

So, what are you waiting for?

Dream big and dream in stereo!

Carpe diem, Baby!

"The best way to predict the future is to create it."

– Peter F. Drucker

Reading and Listening Exploration

- *Women All Over the World – It's Your Time* by Dr. Metashar Dillon
- *What Do You Do with an Idea?* By Kobi Yamada, Mae Besom (children's book but inspiring and encouraging for adults as well)
- *The Tipping Point: How Little Things Can Make a Big Difference* by Malcolm Gladwell
- *Start Something That Matters* by Blake Mycoskie
- *Laws of Success: 12 Laws That Turn Dream Into Reality* by Les Brown
- *NextLevelLeadershipBlog.com and Next Level Leadership Facebook Group* by Chad Schapiro and Marwan Powell
- *No Limits* - Podcast by Rebecca Jarvis
- *Failing Up: How To Take Risks, Aim Higher, and Never Stop Learning* by Leslie Odom, Jr.

Lesson 2

Say It, Write It, Do It

"Dare to say out loud what it is you want,
write it in big bold letters,
and make a plan to do it.
It's your dream. Go live it."

-Andrea Jeffress

Say It

Once you have dared to dream and figured out your "Why", you have speak it into existence and breathe life into your dreams. There is something to be said about voicing a desire out loud rather than in silence that makes it more real and tangible like it really could come true. Perfect examples of two parents who were not afraid to voice their dreams out loud were Richard Williams and LaVar Ball.

Everyone thought Richard Williams was off his rocker when he talked about his daughters becoming incredible tennis players. I remember watching him on TV and reading his braggadocios poster boards telling us how great his kids were now and how great they

were going to be. In fact, he said both would be #1 in the world –
literally willing the future into the present. We all raised an eyebrow
or maybe chuckled then. But who is laughing now. No one. Now it
is hard not to know who Venus and Serena Williams are, and they
are every bit the legends as he said they would be.

People felt the same way about LaVar Ball when it came to his sons,
Lonzo, LiAngelo, and LaMelo. He boldly told his predictions as he
had guided and trained his boys from young ages just like Richard
Williams. Those gentlemen and their wives were the only ones that
could see their own visions, and they exercised their license to speak
their dreams into existence fearlessly.

Now, suffice it to say, we are not all cut out to adopt that bravado
style, and we should be true to ourselves and our own personalities.
While some parents are content to express the desires of our hearts
as muffled whispers, some parents will be unafraid to unleash their
dreams with a cocky confidence and loud brashness that might
throw us into culture shock. Maybe we will never get used to such
brazen intention; yet, it will always be oddly refreshing, and we will
never get enough of it.

Whatever visceral reaction it provokes in us or whatever personality
we might have, the fact of the matter and the take home message is
clear. Whatever our own personal style – quiet or loud…under the
radar or into stratosphere – we must embrace being "Disruptive
Innovators" when it comes to our children, an indeed, our own
selves. Do not be afraid to travel a different road and disrupt a sport
or an industry with our dreams for our children. We should all learn
the power of intention, believing and possessing a willingness to
speak our dreams into existence. Of course, there will be some
naysayers, some hecklers, some non-believers, but pay them no
mind. As Mark Twain wisely said,

"Keep away from people who belittle your ambitions. Small people always do that, but the really great make you feel that you, too, can become great." – Mark Twain

An updated version of this thought was captured in a post by a popular social media personality – Jamie Bennett, The Lifestyle Strategist. Her social media post read:

"STOP ASKING BLIND PEOPLE TO PROOF READ YOUR VISION."

Not everyone will believe in the vision the way you do, not everyone will agree with the way you go about executing your vision or be or be supportive, but it's not their dream to understand. It is your own dream to live.

There are many books and resources that give advice and secrets about how to be intentional about belief. The bible was one of the first resources to discuss this definitively. One of the most poignant scriptures is "Death and life are in the power of the tongue: and they that love it shall eat the fruit thereof" (Proverbs 18:21). You must make it a habit to consciously proclaim everything that God has in store for your life because it is meant for you and only you. You have to be clear and intentional with what you speak because words have power.

Stop right now and say out loud what it is you are dreaming.

When you do this exercise, remember that God says you can have anything you say. So be careful of the power of the tongue. Words are powerful, and prayer is even more powerful. "And whatever you ask in prayer, you will receive, if you have faith" (Matthew 21:22).

You have to have faith that the dream you thought about can come to fruition. If you don't believe, nobody else will.

Write it

After you say your dreams out loud, the next step is to put pen to paper and write down the dream. As the scripture says, "Write the vision and make it plain on tablets, that he may run who reads it" (Habakkuk 2:2). You have to be willing to think about the dream concretely and realistically enough to plan it out. Writing out the plan makes it more likely that you will act upon it.

Recording the dream requires vision and foresight. Sandra Brown is a mother of two sons, Shannon and Sterling, who play professional and collegiate basketball. She wrote an insightful article in Black Enterprise Magazine about the concept of vision. The article begins with the definition of vision - "the act or power of imagination, a supernatural appearance that conveys a revelation" (Merriam-Webster 2016). The article goes on to explore the exercise of creating a personal vision statement.

One way to create a vision statement for yourself was outlined by Jack Canfield in his book, *The Success Principles*, which lists the components of a comprehensive personal vision statement:

- What is your purpose?
- What is your life's dream?
- What are your core values and beliefs?
- What do you want for yourself?
- What do you want to contribute to others?
- What you want to be?

This exercise can be modified to a create a personal academic and athletic vision for your student-athlete and family. This is a great exercise that you can do with your student-athlete using the SMART JOCKS Workbook and Planner 2018-2019 Edition.

Do it

Once you say what you want and write the plan for how you're going to do it, you need to be intentional about the process. You need to think beyond the dream and act on that dream. Everyone has a genius and the power to create the life they want for themselves if they work for it. Whether your dream involves shooting the winning basket, scoring the winning goal, acing your math test, or even being the best version of yourself; your dreams are within your reach.

The first step is deciding what your dream is and what you are willing to do to achieve it. The key is to practice actions that will get you closer to achieving this dream. As some say, practice makes perfect. Practicing good habits and instilling them in your children can get you closer to achieving greatness. Even simple things like taking an extra 30 minutes to practice a specialty shot or looking up extra homework problems to practice for an exam can help you towards excelling at your goals. As you start making little steps to making your vision possible, your dream becomes more tangible.

"When you want to succeed as bad as you want to breathe, then you will be successful." – Eric Thomas

To sum it up, dare to say out loud what it is you want, write it down in big bold letters, and make a plan to do it! You will have be disciplined to concede some major sacrifices for your dreams to come true. It may not happen overnight. You will stumble and have setbacks and failures; however, never lose sight of your dream. You will have to possess an insane, illegal, and inconceivable amount of inner strength, heart and resolve to keep your eye on the goal. Like Eric Thomas says, when you want it as bad as the air you need to breathe, then you will be successful. You will soon find, when you set your heart and mind on something, anything is possible.

Reading and Listening Exploration

- *The Power of Intention* by Dr. Dwayne W. Dyer
- *The Success Principles: How to Get from Where You Are to Where You Want to Be* by Jack Canfield and Janet Switzer
- *Remember You're A Genius Again* by Greg E. Hill
- *On the Line* by Serena Williams and Daniel Paisner
- *Open* by Andre Agassi
- *Shooting Stars* by Buzz Basinger and LeBron James
- *The Secret to Success: When You Want to Succeed as Bad as You Want to Breathe* by Eric Thomas
- *Good Success: Visions and Legacies That Last* by Dr. Metashar Dillon

Create a Winning Blueprint

"It is what it is. But it will be what you make it."

- Pat Summitt

What is a Blueprint?

The definition of a blueprint is a detailed plan or program of action. Consider a blueprint like a map used to reach a destination or treasure or think of it like an architect's drawing of exactly how to build out the home of your dreams. Blueprints can be quite simple or remarkably detailed and are extremely critical to help you become the person you dream of or create the life you want to live. The first step to creating a winning blueprint is to strategize and plan by setting goals.

Set Your Goals and Crush Them

Start by figuring out the end goal and then design a strategy to get there. This may require that you figure out "the lay of the land". You have to become familiar with academic and athletic systems. Each academic component and each athletic component will be unique to everyone.

In creating this blueprint, you must make sure that you are planning on both the academic side and the athletic side within your family or an organization. You cannot create a plan in a vacuum. Naturally, the plan starts with the parent or mentor. You then need all parties - family members, the administration, the teachers, coaches, trainers, community resources, and the student athlete - involved in the planning process. Aim to get buy-in from all team members so everyone will be working towards common goals. You must know your child's learning level and figure out what learning level resources are needed to succeed. Don't be afraid to get help.

The institution's goal should be congruent with the goals set for the student. For example, your administrators should want to have the excellent academic program. You should want to be a part of an excellent academic program. Coaches want to have an excellent academic program. From the administration, coaches, and the parent you all have congruent goals for your student-athlete to excel academically or at the bare minimum maintain eligibility by maintaining a 2.5 GPA. You can do this by talking with academic counselors and knowing the requirements. Once you know what you want to accomplish in academics, you can set a schedule that will help to ensure that you meet your goal.

Becoming familiar with the athletic system means you want to find out the level at which you want to start. Whether you want to start at a YMCA league, a church league, your school team, local team, or local, regional, or national travel basketball team. This can help you and your team to determine how competitive you would like your student-athlete to be.

This is all predicated on what your goals are. When we start to talk about goals, goals are qualitative generalized statements for what you want to accomplish. For example, you may want to make the team; you may want to start; you may want to lead the team in a certain statistical category, like highest in scoring; goals are very personal.

Goals should be developed based on mutually agreed outcomes that want to be achieved. If you are the parent or coach, you should sit with your student athlete and discuss goals in which you both believe that can be achieved. Some goals should be easy to attain some goal should be reach goals. Some goals should be short-term goals, mid-range goals, and long-term goals. Some goals should be standard and based on the skill levels that define proficiency in a given sport. Some goals should then be tailored individually to improve weaknesses and build upon strengths. Some should be easily attainable, and some should be reach goals.

Therefore, you might want to have a tutor, trainer, or coach work with the student-athlete before they get into competitive leagues. If your objective is to have your player ready by a certain period of time than you need to start as soon as possible.

Regarding academics, you still need to set goals. For example, your goal could be to make the Dean's list this year, which is a 3.0 or higher. The next step is to create tactics or strategies on how you are going to accomplish those goals, such as get a tutor to help in certain courses or spending two hours every day on reading and studying. You must allocate time within your day to be successful. Since this objective was measurable, you'll go back and look at those goals and evaluate if you met your goals and even got accomplished some of those reach goals at the end of the semester.

This blueprint is dynamic for both academic and athletic goals and objectives. Dynamic means that things change. As you accomplish goals, you check off those boxes in perhaps add new goals. Setting new goals means that you're always reaching for higher heights.

Create a Schedule and Become a Master Planner – Don't Procrastinate

Once you establish your goals, you need to create a schedule and be disciplined in keeping the schedule. Try to pick a consistent time to set the schedule, like the Saturday or Sunday before the start of the week.

To do this, you must morph into a genius master planner by adopting the attitude that no one should ever out plan you. To become proficient at planning, you must push past the urge to put off today what you could do tomorrow. If you are guilty of this, raise your hands with us and then join us to commit to getting better in this area.

Procrastination is a dream killer and sabotages the planning process. Tips to avoiding procrastination are to use an organizer like the "SMART JOCKS Workbook and Planner" which serves as a dream-catcher journal while reading along with the book. The workbook/planner also functions as a calendar to keep track of all your significant academic and athletic responsibilities. Conquer procrastination and disorganization by logging important tasks like homework, research papers, tests, quizzes, group projects, services hours, game schedules, practice times, nutrition and fitness sessions, camps and showcase schedules, team huddles, family meetings, training webinars/videos and more! Plan out your to do list for important logistics such as hotels, meals, transportation, and equipment inventory and maintenance for your academic and athletic travel calendar. Get reminders for critical deadlines to shake the habit of procrastination and crush your grades and your goals.

Shaking the procrastination monkey off your back gets you on the right track when it comes to setting your goals and strategic plan for the year. It also assures that you make sure you finish what you start – on time and with excellent quality.

Smartphones as mentioned above and computer digital scheduling resources like Google calendar are very helpful. The schedule has five areas that require adequate planning in order for the student athlete to be successful:

- Academics
- Skills Training
- Cardio, Strength & Conditioning
- Nutrition Planning
- Competition scheduling
- Mentoring/volunteer service

Academic planning can be done by using the school academic calendar and class syllabus for each class. Record quiz and test dates, research paper deadlines, tutor and support meetings, standardized testing days, and vacation days to help with planning academic help or training times. For older students, it is also important to schedule out your academic course by using the NCAA

Clearinghouse checklist to make sure you are meeting all the academic requirements each year to meet eligibility requirements.

Scheduling athletic training time can be a daunting task because you have to schedule enough time for skills acquisition, strength and conditioning, and set aside time for the physical trainer for rehab or preventative therapy visits. In sports, it seems an intuitive rule - the person who is practicing more is more likely going to do better. Most people are familiar with Malcolm Gladwell's *"Outliers"* where he discusses the "10,000 Hour Rule", which is a principle that states that "10,000 hours of deliberate practice are needed to become world class in any field (ref)". A new Princeton study dispels this popular premise with a new meta-analysis of 88 studies on deliberate practice. The researcher showed that practice accounted for just 12% difference in performance in various domains, such as games (26%), music (21%), sports (18%), education (4%), and professions (1%).

According to Frans Johansson's book "The Click Rule", this practice principle likely holds truer in domains where the rules are stable and do not change (ref). In areas like entrepreneurship, the rule of 10,000 hours does not hold true. So, let's continue to acknowledge that while the number of hours of practice matters, it may also be quality of practice and not just quantity.

There is a limited amount of time in the day. Students need to allocate hours for academic study, athletic skills training, strength and conditioning, proper nutrition, competition, and mentoring and volunteer service time. This also may include tutors or academic support, athletic trainers, strength and conditioning time, or mentoring and volunteer service time. The schedule also must include time set aside to plan proper nutrition because you have to make time to eat properly in order to have enough fuel to accomplish your objectives.

Be Self-Disciplined

John Maxwell said it best: "At the core of all success principles is self- discipline. There are no quick fixes. It's uphill all the way. Self-discipline is the vehicle that gets you there. There is nothing I can do for an undisciplined person to make them successful."

You have to be disciplined with the schedule. The schedule is an important part of the blueprint because there is a timeline required to accomplish the goals and outcomes. There will be many times when you want to socialize instead of sticking to the calendar, but then you have to keep in mind the goals that have been set. There is very little that can be done for the person who has no self-control to adhere to the tasks that need to get done. It's unrealistic to set goals that cannot be achieved because you do not have the discipline to stick to the plan. As the famous saying goes:

"Do what you gotta do, so you can do what you wanna do."

— Denzel Washington

When the schedule is demanding, time management skills become key. When you exercise good time management skills you will find more freedom from the pressure of deadlines and significantly less stress. You will procrastinate less and have less anxiety. You will also have more time to relax.

Some tips that are useful for time management include the following as outlined by author Donna White:

- Make a list - Lists are no good unless you use them; It is helpful to set reminder alerts on your smartphone or computer to keep track of tasks.

- Set deadlines - Avoid the habit of setting deadlines and then making the decision to push them back; make the deadline a few days before it is actually due. This leaves room for other distractions but still allows enough time to get things down.

- Focus - It is a myth that multi-taskers get more done. It is not always efficient if you are doing to many things at once. Sometimes it is better to allow your mind to focus on one thing at a time. You may find that you consistently finish what you start on a more consistent basis.

- Delegate responsibilities - Do not be a control freak. You cannot do everything. You have to find people you trust and who are competent that you can assign a task or a project to help you get things done. That may also mean that you give your child more responsibility for their own lives. This will help with the maturity process as well.

- Use your free time wisely - Although it's good to relax during your downtime like in the doctor's office, during a train commute, on a lunch break, etc. Sometimes you can use this time to plan out the next day, the meal plan, the game schedule, transportation, etc. This doesn't have to be all the time because you want to avoid burnout. It does improve efficiency.

- Reward yourself - Celebrate your wins in a safe and healthy way! But do not let the celebration get in the way of maintaining your schedule to continue to meet your goals.

Take the Initiative

Another step in creating a winning blueprint is to learn to take the initiative and be self-motivated. Not only should we be ingraining this idea into our children, but as adults, we should be adopting this attitude ourselves, taking this lesson to heart.

Initiative is the wonderful ability to think, assess and act alone and independently. For parents, there may be a time where you are not around to motivate, organize, schedule, transport, and, certainly not, perform for your child. For students, there may be times when no one is around to motivate you to get your studies done or your workouts in - not your parent, your mentor, your teacher, friends or your coach. In these instances, you must have the initiative to do what it takes to stay on course to accomplish your goals without anyone reminding you, henpecking you, brow-beating you, or begging you to do so. You will have to rely your maturity, self-discipline, time-management skills, organizational know-how, imagination and common sense to get done what needs to be done. You are the only one responsible for you so take the initiative.

Be Self-Motivated

In addition to having the motor of a self-starter, we have to learn ways to stay self-motivated. This is a challenge because motivation waxes and wanes. This is not an uncommon phenomenon. As Zig Ziglar, the great American motivator once said,

"People say motivation doesn't last. Well, neither does bathing. That's why we recommend it daily."

- Zig Ziglar

Although we have faith in the process and believe in what the future will hold, sometimes it is hard to remain motivated when you cannot see the reward right in front of you. We live in an immediate gratification culture; and often, if we do not see the fruits of our labor right away, we get discouraged. In his sermons and books, Bishop TD Jakes talks about even strong people need gentle encouragement sometimes.

The trick to staying motivated is to know your personality and your "love language" to find out what best motivates you. Based on your personality and personal circumstance, finding ways to stay encouraged and remain on task can come in many forms, such as inspirational talks or quotes, videos or podcasts, books, mediation and prayer, prizes and rewards.

Rewards and prizes can include verbal praise, monetary awards, time off or vacation, clothing or equipment gifts, or pampering like massages or manicures/pedicures, etc. Whether it be material or monetary, if you have done this on occasion, no judgement here. We all have. This may seem like bribery for our kids to do well. However, recognize that this is not always practical or ideal and should not be a regular occurrence. The main reason parents should not make this a habit is that the kids must develop their own drive outside of a promised reward.

The exception acceptable motivational tools to is violence - mental or physical. We do not condone the use of violence as a means to motivate, teach, or control a child or adult. Parents, if you were raised this way, you have to do some soul-searching and find another way. Violence begets violence and if you do not stop, the cycle never will.

To conclude, the take home message to both parents and children in this chapter is to create a winning blueprint through goal setting and planning. The next step is to develop the self-discipline to maintain a schedule that focuses not just your athletics, but on your academics as well. Show poise, leadership, and maturity by taking the initiative in carrying out responsibilities on your own and be accountable for reaching your own goals and dreams. Finally, learn to find ways to stay motivated with intention and wisdom so that you develop good practice habits while staying recharged and refueled and keeping your eye on the ultimate prize – success on the field and success in life.

So, set aside some time today to create your winning blueprint. It will be well worth the investment.

Reading and Listening Exploration

- *SOAR: Build Your Vision from the Ground Up!* by T.D. Jakes
- *The Outliers: The Story of Success* by Malcolm Gladwell
- *Make the Impossible Possible: One Man's Crusade to Inspire Others to Dream Bigger and Achieve the Extraordinary* by Bill Strickland with Vince Rause
- *Awaken the Giant Within: How to Take Immediate Control of Your Mental, Emotional, Physical and Financial Destiny!* by Tony Robbins
- *The Five Love Languages: The Secret to Love That Lasts* by Gary Chapman
- *The Five Love Languages of Teenagers: The Secret to Love That Lasts* by Gary Chapman
- *Zig Ziglar's Little Instruction Book: Inspiration and Wisdom from America's Top Motivator* by Zig Ziglar
- *SMART JOCKS Workbook and Planner 2018-2019 Edition* by Andrea and William Jeffress (website)

Lesson 4

Invest in Your Future

"The question is not whether we can afford to invest in every child; it is whether we can afford not to."

-Marian Wright Edelman

Big Business

Sports is big business and has been since ancient times. Today, in fact, the empire of sports is a multi-billion-dollar industry. Immersing your children in sports is no easy feat, especially in the current era of "pay to play".

The effort to gain a competitive edge has kids starting at such a younger age now, and instead of playing many sports, they are choosing to master one sport rather than many to keep the cost of participation down. Two of the biggest costs are travel and equipment improvement costs. For example, football helmets can cost from $65 - $650. Baseball and softball bats can run a parent up to $300. Teams as young as 1st, 2nd and 3rd grade are traveling to AAU tournaments in different states, which increases the cost of travel and lodging, often making it cost prohibitive for some students to join travel teams.

> *"The bar isn't the only thing that's being hit hard and amateur sports these days; bank accounts are, too. Increasingly, there is a price to play, both for the parents of youth athletes and for the adults who take to the field themselves. Sports are no longer just about the numbers of runs, goals, points, hits and assists. The competitiveness that takes place, even at the amateur level, comes with the rising cost of camps, equipment, travel, tournaments, uniforms and venues."* – David Greisman

It is this competitiveness that takes place at the amateur level has caused the cost of participation to spiral out of control. This financial crisis for parents is discussed in a book on the rising cost of youth sports entitled, *"The Most Expensive Game in Town"* written by Mark Hyman, a Baltimore journalist. He profoundly observes, "Businesses understand that parents are vulnerable, they have dreams and aspirations for their kids. They have figured that out, leveraged that and are capitalizing financially on it."

Given the tantalizing entertainment value of sports, the funding that is required to compete even on a basic level, not to mention on an elite level, can be daunting. Some of the more expensive sports such as golf, football, baseball, hockey, tennis, ice-skating, dancing, skiing or fencing, to name a few, can be difficult to continue without having the means to fund the investment. We also know these sports are often more expensive than others because of the rental space, activity fees like court time or ice time, the gear and/or the team coaching and private coaching required to gain a mastery of skills to dominate a sport. Basketball or track on the other hand has less cost associated in it due to the outdoor accessibility of places to play and train. Even so, these sports are expensive as you go further up the chain of travel basketball and AAU due to the travel and tournament scheduling.

Unless a child is fortunate to make it to a sponsored team level like grassroots sponsored events such as Under Armour, Adidas, Nike, or other corporate sponsored teams, this cost is incurred by the parent, family members, mentors or coaches. It's not uncommon for a family to spend $300-$500 per child and up to $1,000 - $10,000 per person, per household, per year in sports-related fees. One friend of ours whose name we will not reveal confided in us that she spent close to $30,000 in one year for travel and hotel fees dedicated to her children's participation in travel sports. Between all the activity fees, lessons costs, venue rental, tournament entry fees, camps, uniforms and equipment, travel costs, hotel and food bills, athletic trainer sessions, strength and conditioning sessions, medical/therapy copays and deductibles, the fees can skyrocket quickly. Many programs would not be able to run without local sponsorships and fundraisers to offset the burden from the parents and coaching staff.

Without a significant financial contribution from family, the never-ending duties of fundraising, or the gracious generosity of benefactors and sponsors, financing the dream is often the rate-limiting step. If you cannot get past the funding obstacles, it is difficult to make it out of the starting blocks and over the first, second or last hurdle. Although having limited resources makes it difficult to finish, it does not make it impossible.

Create a Spending Plan and Commit to Fundraise

Creating a spending plan and committing to fundraising is a key component in implementing the blueprint to get ahead of the competition. Unless you are independently wealthy, money can be a stressor so most times it takes some creative funding and fundraising to make this dream a reality. Oftentimes if you show the commitment to develop your potential, other people will come to your aid. You may have the great fortune to have some guardian angels come along to assist you with some of the financial burden. We have been very fortunate to have the help of our family and friends so many times, which has been a Godsend. Of course, you can't depend on it, and you always have to remember to have a spirit of gratitude when it does come.

In addition to the help of family and friends, most parents are assigned fundraising duties throughout the year. Of course, there are the traditional ways of fundraising such as raffles, merchandise sales, car washes, bake sales, Chinese auctions, coupon books, specialty event fundraisers, etc. However, the other way to raise money is by using popular crowdfunding sites or social media platforms, a modern and popular way to raise funds for your child as an individual or as a team. Our Global Vision, an online internet mall, was a wonderful platform that I have used as an affiliate marketer in the past which was donating a portion of proceeds to charity through its Amazon "SWAG BUCKS". I am sure there are many other programs out there with this same promotion.

You can also apply for individual sports grants and school grants to enable activities for kids focusing on the benefits of physical activity and health and wellness and children. If your organization directly serves youths between the ages of 3 and 18 as an organized sport, recreational activity, or fitness program, you may be eligible to apply for youth sports sponsorships. Many sports brands and corporate sponsors desire to inspire positive social change at a grass roots level by providing funding support to develop curriculum for nonprofit sports programs.

Aside from fundraising and sports grants, the best way to cope with limited resources is to bootstrap your training and take a cooperative, collective approach to athletics. This means to avoid thinking of yourself as an island and learn to work cooperatively with your family, friends and community to get the training services, equipment and expertise you need to not only survive the process of athletic development, but flourish.

Create a Spending Plan – not a Budget

Many people don't even bother creating a monthly budget, and if they make one, they do not stick to it. Mark Hyman remarks, "Parents won't compromise no matter how tight their budget is." He goes on to say, "They'll still have their kids playing. They still manage to fork out $300, $400 for their kids to play sports. As a parent, you always want to do more for your kids than what you had." We've all been that parent, right? Even though we are aware that this lack of budget consciousness is not healthy, we still succumb to being somewhat reckless to chase the dream.

We as parents have to become more financially literate to make our children's dreams a reality. We can break this cycle by creating a sheet for a monthly spending plan – a concept adapted from a book called *"Money Does Matter and So Does How You Handle It"* by Dr. Chandra Winford. In her book, she does a nice job explaining how to create your monthly spending plan. She calls it a spending plan instead of a budget because it is less restrictive in our minds. It is more realistic approach because, after all, in our minds, we are going to spend what we want to spend and how we want to spend it so that our kids have the very best. So, let's not pretend we are not going to spend the money – rather let's realistically plan how we are going to spend the money we need to get Johnny to his race with the best sneakers on. If we don't have the money on our spending plan, then at least we know there is a short fall and we know we have to take it from somewhere else and fundraise to go get it.

A monthly spending plan should include everything that you foresee spending in a month. The easiest way to do this is to use an Excel spreadsheet on your mobile phone or computer. Try to be honest and put a realistic estimate. This will help you keep track of trends and assist you in setting spending priorities.

Of course, paying yourself first should be on the top of the list in the category of savings, followed by your debts because you want to get out of debt as quickly as possible. Being debt free and maintaining good credit is a bucket list goal, and in all transparency, many of us are struggling with this – so do not feel alone. You can always seek further detailed assistance with a personal accountant, certified financial planner, insurance agent or debt recovery specialist as we could all use some encouragement and specialized advice on the subject of financial literacy.

Here is a blank spending plan worksheet with a list of line items and bill categories as adopted from Dr. Winford's book above. There are columns to keep track of the due date for bills, the bill amounts, the pay period date, and salary amount. Keep in mind that no parentheses around a number means a positive surplus, and parentheses around a number would indicate a shortage.

Items to include on the Monthly Spending Worksheet:

Net Pay – insert the amount of your check per pay period
Bill Categories & Total Expenses

- Savings/Emergency Fund - list the amount to save per pay period
- Mortgage (s) / Rent fees
- Credit Card(s)
- Loan(s)
- Car payment(s)
- Insurance: Car(s)
- Insurance: Home(s)
- Insurance: Health
- Insurance: Disability – long-term / short-term policies
- Utilities: Electric
- Utilities: Gas
- Utilities: Water
- Utilities: Sewer
- Utilities: Cable/Internet
- Phone (s): Cell/Land Line
- Food/Groceries
- Gasoline – cars and lawn equipment
- Healthcare Costs – copays, prescriptions, dental, eye
- Entertainment – travel, dining out, activities
- Personal Care – pedicures/manicures, haircuts, massages
- Maintenance: Car/Home – consider separate emergency fund
- Hotel Fees
- Transportation Fees
- Equipment/Clothing
- Activity Fees/Tournament Fees
- Miscellaneous: Non-Routine Costs
- Subscriptions/Memberships – Newspapers/Magazines/Gym/Work

DRS. ANDREA AND WILLIAM JEFFRESS

Date: _____ Monthly Spending Plan Worksheet Template			
Bills	Due Date	Pay Date	Pay Date
Net Pay			
Savings/ Emergency Fund			
Mortgage (s)/ Rent fees			
Credit Card (s)			
Loan(s)			
Car Payment(s)			
Insurance: Car/Home Health/Disability			
Utilities: Sewer/Gas Electric/C&I/Water			
Phone (cell/land line)			
Food/Groceries			
Gasoline			
Healthcare Costs			
Entertainment			
Personal Care			
Maintenance: Car/Home			
Hotel Fees			
Transportation Fees			
Equipment/ Clothing			
Activity Fees/ Tourney Fees			
Misc: Non-Routine Costs			
Subscriptions/Memberships			
Total Expenses			

No parentheses = Surplus / Parentheses ( ) = Shortage

As the cost of participation in sports continues to increase, parents need to commit to this exercise in financial literacy and budgeting to make our goals and dreams a reality.

"I don't think it is an exaggeration to say that the financial literacy, economic empowerment and wealth building is going to be the last leg of the civil rights movement. Because one step toward financial literacy takes you two steps towards personal empowerment."

— Russell Simmons

Be Resourceful

After you have budgeted - ahem...excuse us - created your spending plan on how you are going the allocate the money you bring into the household, you also must find ways to be resourceful to make ends meet and stay within your spending plan.

One example is how we did this with our oldest daughter, Adrianna, in tennis. Tennis is a crazy expensive sport. To make it more affordable, we took advantage of bundled tennis lesson packages - for example, buy 9 up front and get the 10th lesson free. Our primary coach, Head Pro Ric Harden at Westwood Tennis and Racquet Center, organized small group lessons for tennis with some of her peers to share the lesson cost with another family. We also found hitting partners that were top level college students. We needed hitting partners and they needed cash in their pockets. It was a win-win situation. I picked up more tennis balls than you have ever imagined over the course of the years to save time for pick up during the lesson, so she could hit more balls. We bought used rackets, until we could afford new ones. We bartered teaching the younger classes during staffing crunches for extra court time or use of the ball machine. I called equipment companies, like On Court Off Court and spoke to the guy on the tennis channel, the venerable Coach Joe Dinoffer, who was so kind as to give us discounts on large bulk orders on supplies as we also used them for the grassroots program at Burton Park as well. We drove instead of flying. We carpooled with other parents. We used the travel websites to bid for rooms at low cost and often stayed at budget motels. We just had one bad hotel in all those years and that was the one Adrianna refused to stay in due to the presence of bugs and prostitutes - so I checked out immediately with no refund - lol.

In basketball and volleyball, we did much of the same. We have participated in a myriad of fundraisers. We have carpooled with other parents. We have slept over friends' homes to save on the cost of hotels. William has slept at home of the former Mr. Basketball of Ohio, Coach Sonny Johnson, head of Northeast Ohio Elite Youth Basketball. When he was 14, William slept in his daughter's barbie bed with the feet of his 6'5'' frame dangling way off the edge of the bed. Man, I wish I had a picture of that now! It would be serious blackmail!

The moral of the story is - chasing your dream is doable by making a spending plan and being budget conscious and resourceful. The dream is attainable - but you have to find a way to make it affordable. You can't be afraid to make some sacrifices and some concessions along the way. These sacrifices pay big dividends.

Return on Investment

With all of this hard work and financial sacrifice, we all wonder whether it will be worth it. We think about it like an investment in our future, but what is going to be the return on our investment? To talk about return on investment we need to understand what dividends are.

A dividend is a cash payment made by a corporation to its shareholders as a profit distribution from the company. Sometimes these payouts are given as more stock instead. In other words, if you invest in a company, hopefully it makes money, a profit, and you'll get all your money back and then some. Let's look at this comparison further.

When people invest in the stock market, we are usually advised to invest wisely, but without fear. We buy a stock in a company where we are going to place our money and make sure that it's a company that is going to do well with potential to grow. The company is our child. So, we invest our heart and soul into the company and watch it grow. We hold on to the stock of the company for a long time. Warren Buffet, the CEO of Berkshire Hathaway, widely known as one of the greatest investors of all times, has an investment philosophy that says, "If you don't feel comfortable owning stock for over 10 years, you shouldn't own it for 10 minutes." He believes in holding on to a stock for a long time to allow the price to continue to grow before selling it to make a profit. In his world, patience is a virtue. He once said, "Our favorite holding period is forever." In other words, he buys the stock at a low price, holds onto it a long time, and the money compounds, growing exponentially. It's like waiting to eat a green banana until its golden yellow. After the stock is ripe, he sells it for a much higher price than what he bought for which makes him and his partners, or shareholders, even more wealthy than they already are. The cash profit the company makes and gives back to its shareholders over a time period is called a dividend.

We can apply this same philosophy in our investment in sports. Parents invest in their child's future with the hope of reaping a great return. In the analogy above the dividend was cash, but that is not always the case. There are many non-monetary rewards that can be reaped for a child have a lifelong love affair with sports.

Whatever the reward, funding a child's dream will take resourcefulness and patience. And just like the stock market, our talent needs time to grow - so you must hold steady and do not sell your stock at the first sign of trouble, instability, or adversity. You should hold steady a long time through the good and bad periods - the stock price is going to have times when it jumps high or drops low. Now, that is not to say throw money away. If you have no talent, no dedication, self-discipline or work ethic, then you must re-evaluate your investment. Warren Buffet also once said, "If you find yourself in a hole, stop digging". With that said, investing in your child's shared dream and vision is a game where you need to have patience and a long-term plan, perseverance, strength and resolve. If you start early, the money invested in your child's talent could pay dividends with a solid return on your investment.

For us, our investment paid off big time. Adrianna, the oldest, was a tennis player, the dividend was approximately $160,000 after graduating Magna Cum Laude with a 3.88 GPA from Mercyhurst University debt free. She played four years with a partial athletic NCAA Division II scholarship and then covered her academics under a tuition exchange program. For our middle daughter Jasmine, investing in travel volleyball taught her the focus and discipline she needed to complete the International Baccalaureate Program at Mercyhurst Preparatory School and earn a year worth of college credits.

So, instead of her entering her sophomore year at Robert Morris University, she is now actually in her junior year. She has continued to play club volleyball at RMU and used her leadership skills that she learned on the court to land a dorm resident assistant job to earn her room and board next year. So, between her resident assistant job and tuition exchange from faculty work at Mercyhurst University, she is going to finish college debt free and on track to graduate one year early - a savings of approximately $97,500 in tuition and room and board costs over 4 years. Finally, William, the youngest, a rising sophomore in high school and basketball standout at McDowell High School already has Division I basketball offers that include a one and done clause - meaning even if you leave to enter the NBA draft, you can still get a discounted education. By the time William gets to college, we predict it's going to cost upwards to $200,000 to go to college.

In the end it's about what the return on your investment will be. If you are going to play a sport, you really must be committed to it or you are wasting a great deal of money for absolutely nothing. If you are going to college, you still need do your part outside of the coaches recruiting you like filling out your FAFSA financial aid form in a timely fashion to make sure you are eligible to take advantage of certain grants which are time sensitive and fall outside your scholarship. And that could prevent you from going to school because you did not fill out your financial aid forms properly and in a timely fashion.

Perhaps even college is not for you and want to pursue a trade. If you do not want to go to a 4-year institution or the military, then, definitely investigate a trade! Trade workers are making top dollars! And many other the positions with these high wage earners go unfilled. So, you could use sports to propel you into a vocational school where you may still pursue your athletic career. Whatever the choice, make your investment plan work for you. Dr. Boyce Watkins states, "One thing that's true is that whether you are making a financial investment or an investment of the heart, you usually get what you give. What's also true is that investing the wrong assets into the wrong places is a great way to end up broke (or broken)."

Looking at our situation, our dreams came true on the most basic level of using athletics as a means to pursue higher education in an economical way that provides our children a way to be debt free. The return on our investment will be $473,000 minus what we put in to each child to train them. Considering that three college educations will be secured - it is absolutely worth it - every ounce of hard work, every tear, every loss, every fight, every nagging injury, every dashed hope, every disappointment… gave way to a win.

And it was all worth it.

Reading and Listening Exploration

- *Money Does Matter and So Does How You Handle It* by Chandra Winford.
- *Rich Dad Poor Dad* by Robert Kiyosaki and Sharon Lechter
- *Black Millionaires of Tomorrow* by Dr. Boyce Watkins
- *The Dave Ramsey Show* by Ramsey Solutions on Apple Podcasts
- *"Think and Grow Rich"* by Napoleon Hill; later edition – Napoleon Hill and Dennis Kimbro
- *The Money Book for the Young, Fabulous & Brokee* by Suze Orman

Lesson 5

Build a Team

"If you want to run fast, run alone;
if you want to run far, run together."

-African Proverb

W e have weaved the philosophy of this African proverb into the very fabric of our lives. We know without a shadow of a doubt that we are stronger together, but we are only as strong as our weakest link. Our family has mastered running in stride with one another, and we fly like the wind. The famed Coach Phil Jackson summed it up nicely as well. He wisely stated,

"The strength of the team is each individual member.
The strength of each member is the team." – Phil Jackson

Over the years of raising our kids, we have taken this lesson to heart. Surrounding ourselves with the best teachers and the best coaches and building our network with the most resourceful friends has been the key to our success. We understand that only with a good support system and team structure can we go further than if we were to go at it alone.

#SquadGoals

A "**team**" by definition is a number of persons associated together in work or an activity. We are going to define team as a group of people working together to accomplish a common goal. The members work intensely on a specific, common goal using their positive synergy, individual and mutual accountability, and complementary skills.

The primary members of the team will be the parent, guardian, mentor, coach, teacher, counselor, administrator, spiritual advisor or any other support personnel deemed necessary for the student-athlete to be successful. Please note, any one of the team members maybe considered the leader at any given point in time. The leader may be the one who has identified the potential student-athlete as a number one draft pick; therefore, they may be the one that formulates the team and begins the process of putting together the blueprint for success.

We all have #SquadGoals. However, the team is not just there to be our cheerleading squad. Sure, they are there to cheer you on, but they are also there to tell you the things you don't want to hear and push you when you don't really want to be pushed. They are not supposed to coddle you, or shower you with praise constantly, or blow smoke up your butt. The primary job of the team is supposed to be to hold you accountable to do the work that is necessary for you to achieve realistic goals and be within striking distance of your reach goals.

Follow the Leader

Now that we have identified our team members, it is time to choose a leader. A **leader** is someone who can influence others and who has managerial authority. This needs to be clear to prevent problems in the future. Leadership comes down to motivating the people who are on your team and making the right decisions. Sometimes you have to grab onto the coattails of someone else leading and going up because this going to help your son or daughter get better.

The leader of the team will work with the team formulate the student-athlete's vision and mission. It will complete a SWOT analysis (see Chapter 10). A SWOT analysis is an evaluation of the student-athletes strengths, weaknesses, opportunities, and threats in both academics and athletics. This should be a transparent process and include the student-athlete's self-assessment. Once the team has completed its analysis, a blueprint can be created to address ways to make strengths stronger and the weaknesses become strengths.

Leader vs. Leadership

Now that we have identified our team leader and team members and designed a strategic blueprint for success, this is a good time to distinguish between the definition of leader and leadership. Our definition of a leader is someone who can influence others and who has "parental" or "coaching" authority. Leadership is a process of leading the team, making the right decisions, and influencing the student-athlete and the team to achieve its goals. A parent may have authority but may not always be the person who has identified the student-athlete as a number one draft pick. However, the parent has the authority to give the power or leadership role to the person who has identified the student-athlete as a number one draft pick. The parent empowers that individual with the authority to take on a leadership role in order to meet or reach the goals for the student-athlete that has been set by the team. A role refers to behavior patterns (responsibilities) expected of someone occupying a given position on the team. On a team, individuals are expected to do certain things because of their position within the team. These roles are generally oriented towards either getting work done or keeping team members happy.

A team's performance potential depends on the role each individual team member plays and resources each individual is able to bring to the team. These resources include knowledge, abilities, and skills in the areas of academics, athletics, nutrition, health, career, and life in general. That is why we must emphasize the importance of interpersonal skills. Interpersonal skills - especially conflict management and resolution, collaborative problem-solving, and communication consistently emerge as important factors for high performance teams. That is why we are recommending that you identify 2 to 4 people who act as your leadership team. The leadership team's responsibility will be to identify the team members that will play a pivotal role in the success of the student-athlete and they will be the primary decision-makers on the student-athletes behalf.

Assign Team Roles and Organize the Plan

A good way to assign team roles and organize your team is by asking 8 important team building questions using the memory aid: W.H.Y. (Table 1).

In the acronym, W.H.Y. there are 5W's, 2H's, and one "Y". The 5W's are: Who, What, When, Where, Why? The 2H's are: How and How much? The 1 "Y" is yield. These questions assist you in picking your team members, and they also help you to start thinking about how to structure your studying time and training time. Finally, the questions force you to ask how much time and money you are willing to invest in the process.

Table 1.

Questions	8 Team Building Questions to Organize Your Team: W.H.Y.: "5W's -2 H's – 1 Y"
Who?	Family, Friends, Mentors, Churches, Community Members, Coaches, Trainers, Teachers, Counselors Administrators
What?	What are they here to help with? What do they bring to the table?
Where?	Where do I study? Where do I play? Where do I get the assistance I need?
When?	When do I study? When do I play?
Why?	Why am I looking to them for assistance? Why are they helping?
How?	How will I learn? (i.e., by myself, tutor, study group, online, after school, and summer school) How will I train? (i.e., by myself, with a local team, with a regional team, personal trainer, in a group)
How much?	How much time, money, and mental capacity will I decide to invest
Yield?	Can you quantify the results you want your team to yield?

"Coming together is a beginning.
Keeping together is progress.
Working together is success."

– Henry Ford

In conclusion, as the saying goes: "There is no 'I' in TEAM", and you are only as good as the people with which you surround yourself. A great team leader inspires, motivates, and promotes the student athlete and team above him or herself in the best interest of the team. As the great industrialist and car maker and inventor Henry Ford once said, "Coming together is a beginning. Keeping together is progress. Working together is success."

Ultimately, building a team is one thing, but managing the team as a cohesive unit is another. Managing a team that works together to achieve a common goal is a challenging but doable feat. This feat can be accomplished by following a leader who evaluates in order to make the right decisions and builds a team that brings value to the table to make his or her student-athlete grow, develop and shine.

But building a great team is not for the faint at heart. If you are up to the challenge, we encourage you to assemble your team through strategic alliances based on similar goals, valuable skill sets or resources, and a genuine desire to see your student-athlete do well. It's your foundation and key to massive success. Build it well, and triumph will come.

Reading and Listening Exploration

- *LeBron's Dream Team* by LeBron James
- *Lean In: Women Work and the Will to Lead* by Sheryl Sandberg
- *Start with Why: How Great Leaders Inspire Everyone to Take Action* by Simon Sinek
- *The 10X Rule: The Only Difference Between Success and Failure* by Grant Cardone
- *Outliers: The Story of Success by* Malcolm Gladwell
- *The Servant Leader* by James A. Autry

$\mathcal{L}$esson 6

Manage the Process

"Management is doing things right;
leadership is doing the right things."

-Peter F. Drucker

N ow that you have made the right decisions – to dream the dream, say it out loud and write it down, create a winning blueprint, invest in your future, and build a solid team – you need to learn to manage the group so that it works well together and runs smoothly like a finely oiled machine. For the team to do this and accomplish the student's academic and athletic goals, it is important to master the often-unappreciated task of doing things right - the art of management.

The definition of management is the process of working with and through people to achieve personal or organizational goals both efficiently and effectively. To hold people or team members accountable for what you are asking them to do in the areas they are responsible for, you must become expert at balancing the

"P.O.L.E." – an acronym for the four functions of management: **Planning, Organizing, Leading, and Evaluating** to control or improve the outcome.

This is the point where the glamourous lead and the limelight exit stage left, and the tireless, behind the scenes planner and organizer enters stage right. This is the person or people who work hard to get the stuff done in the trenches that no one may ever see, and if it's done well, the operation runs so smoothly that it often gets taken for granted – and hence is underappreciated. A hand clap goes out to all the parents, family members, mentors, booster club or travel team parents, coaches, team administrators, teachers, counselors, and school administrators that are doing this daily to make sure the engine of the process remains in perfect working condition. Management can be a tedious and unpopular job - planning, organizing, leading and critiquing to get better, but we must recognize that managing the process with discipline, positivity, joy and love is absolutely critical to our success.

> *"To be successful, you have to learn to do things you don't like. You find ways to like the process and make the most of that time."* – *Mike Krzyzewski*

Be Accountable

As you began to organize your team, putting the right people in the right place at the right time to help you manage the process is paramount. It is imperative that you identify a leader, assign responsibilities, determine how decisions are going to be made, and communicate who has authority to make decisions.

Now that the leader has been identified, he or she can work with all the other team members to motivate them to accomplish goals. The leader can always delegate leadership responsibility to others in the

SMART JOCKS

support system, but remember, the leader should make the final decision. You are going to have numerous people and personalities vying for the leader's time. That is why whoever is in the leadership role should have excellent leadership characteristics and interpersonal skills.

Ultimately, the leader must follow the plan, organize the people, motivate the people to be accountable for their tasks and constantly evaluate and control their progress. Where there is a weakness, a strategy must be put in place to develop it into a strength. Where there is a strength, a plan must be put in place to capitalize on it to accomplish milestones and outcomes that will continue to set the player a cut above. A leader must have vision and toughness to see and do both.

Be a Problem Solver

The process will never be 100% smooth, so just expect some bumps in the road. It's only natural to come upon some obstacles that need to be overcome. While managing the process, the first thing you need to do is identify the problem. Once the problem is identified, you should come up with alternatives solution to the problem by looking at all the options and resources that you have at your disposable to solve the problem. Do not be afraid to ask for help. This is where networking and seeking out the help of others can be so critical to development of a student athlete or sports professional.

After making the decision to attack the problem, you must ensure that your team is ready to implement the solution(s) and adjust their process. The foundation of effective problem solving is communication and being open and honest about goals, expectations, discipline, and reward. Having open lines of communication is key.

Communicate and Network

We are not here just to be in it, we are here to win it; we are not in it to participate, we are here to dominate. It's not just about hard work, it's about smart work. It's not just about grunt work, it's about your network. We must have great communication with all your team members (parents, guardians, mentors, administrators, coaches, teachers, counselors and any other support persons deemed necessary for the student-athlete to be successful). Everything in the management process involves communication. A manager cannot formulate a strategy or decide without information, which must be communicated. The best leaders stay networked with the team and other community resources who can help the mission.

In today's fast paced world, everyone has a busy schedule. That is why we have utilized several technological advances to address our communication issues. We have put all our kids on a schedule with a shared calendar on Google Docs. I know most of you dread getting your child a mobile phone; however, it has been a lifesaver for us. Everyone has easy access to their calendar. We no longer have to wait around at a practice wondering if they are going to be finished. We can get a text when one of our kids are headed to the locker room, and by the time they have finished changing, we are on our way for to them pick up. This gives us ample time to leave the house and be right on time for pick-up. It also can become very handy if your student-athletes plans change.

You also need to stay in contact with their teachers, coaches, and administrators. It is imperative to go to all parent teacher/coach/administrator conference meetings that you can. This ensures that they are all on board and a part of the team. Most school districts have a learning management system that you can stay in constant contact with them and you will be able to be kept up to date when it comes to homework assignments, quizzes, tests, and grades. The earlier you can intervene on poor performance, the better. There is no reason you cannot stay in constant contact with your team. The key is not to be afraid to embrace technology. The following is a list of some technology you can use:

Wireless Communication – works almost anywhere
- Managers and student athletes "keep in touch" using smartphones, tablet computers, notebook computers, and mobile pocket devices.

Networked Communication Applications – work on Wifi
- **E-mail** — instantaneous transmission of messages that are linked together.
- **Instant Messaging** — interactive, real-time communication that takes place among computer users who are logged on to the computer network at the same time. Information can be communicated instantaneously.
- **Google Voice** — Voicemail system digitizes a spoken message, transmits it over the network, and stores the message on a disk for the receiver to retrieve later.
- **Video/Teleconferencing** — allows a group of people to meet simultaneously using telephone or e-mail group communications software; video conferencing allows for meeting participants to see each other over video screens – for ex: Google Hangouts, Zoom
- **Software and Network Packages** — Email, document sharing, presentation creation and sharing, centralized document storage, and more.
- **Internet** — Email, research, voice communication, group communication, and more.
- **Social Media** — personal connections, branding and marketing, instant messaging applications are now available.
- **Mobile Phone Applications** — use for checking Infinite Campus or other school related technology interfaces, study

skills applications, finance applications, language apps, entertainment apps, music apps, games and more.

Being a competent leader, being disciplined and accountable, problem solving, communicating well, and embracing technology should ease you right into the role of becoming an expert manager who is adept at the planning and organizing process. Team leader(s) need to evaluate the progress with a critical eye, always looking at short and long-term plans and outcomes and adjust the process accordingly. When you create a strategic plan, every member of the team should be accountable to their part of carrying out the initiatives and plans for growth and improvement that were set forth during the planning and organizing process. The leaders and members of the team should be open to being creative and flexible because the plan is dynamic and is constantly changing. The strategy you use to get better and chase your dreams may change, too. Successful individuals, teams, and families like ours learn to "balance the P.O.L.E." and manage this process expertly to grow and thrive beyond their wildest imaginations.

And so can you.

Reading and Listening Exploration

- *The Chick in Charge* by Mary H. Parker
- *The Leadership Challenge* by Kouzes and Posner
- *How to Win Friends and Influence People* by Dale Carnegie
- *The Next Generation of Women Leaders: What You Need to Lead But Won't Learn in Business School* by Selena Rezvani
- *Class is Now in Session...Your 21 LinkedIn Questions Answered* by Tajuana Ross, The LinkedIn Professor

Triple Threat Challenge

Contributor: Adrianna Jeffress

*"My best skill was that I was coachable.
I was a sponge and aggressive to learn."*

- Michael Jordan

The Triple Threat

E very kid deserves a parent, a mentor or a coach who can push them to be good students, good athletes, and good leaders – this makes that child a triple threat. In gridiron football a triple threat athlete is a player who excels at all three skills – running, passing, and kicking. In modern times, such a player is referred to as a utility player. At SMART JOCKS, we made a similar analogy by challenging them to become triple threat student-athletes: academic, athletic, and civic minded.

Becoming a triple threat makes a student-athlete a much more attractive candidate. Being academically strong, athletically talented, and community driven identifies that child or young adult as a well-rounded individual who can lead their team to greater heights. Possessing maturity, leadership and sound situational judgment are other key personal qualities that define a winner. Those are the kids who are become number one draft picks on and off the court.

One way to develop a triple threat is by ensuring that all parties involved understand the direction or the goals that have been set before them. For example, if you would like to be strong academic, then you must project an image of confidence and show a desire to complete the academic work to the same standard as you train on the field. The same thing goes with athletics. Being civic-minded shows that the student-athlete cares about something greater than themselves.

Administrators, coaches, teachers, mentors and parents want to be a part of a winning team. Having a number one draft pick on your team who is a triple threat usually translate into massive wins. The more number one draft picks you have on your team, the more likely your team will win championships. Therefore, it is in the best interest of a school, team, and/or an organization to recruit, retain, and invest in number one draft picks.

Be grateful for Instruction and Feedback

It's important that triple threat students are coachable or teachable. To improve, students must be open to constructive criticism and accept the feedback from their parents and coaches and vice versa. Qualities that make us coachable and teachable are being a good listener, humble, observant, having a good attitude, and open to new ideas and new ways of doing things. Being defensive or combative when listening to feedback about performance, are poor quality traits that lead to labeling a student-athlete un-coachable.

Often when a student-athlete is not coachable, her talent will plateau, and she will stop acquiring more refined skill. However, the person who is grateful to receive the knowledge and the instruction that they have been given is the one whose trajectory keeps going up. That is the individual whose potential continues to be realized.

What's Good for the Goose is Good for the Gander

It is important that parents, coaches, teachers, and administrators be open to constructive criticism and new ideas as well. To improve, we need to be able to accept feedback from all team members. Being open to suggestions is tough for some people. They have the attitude that it is their way or the highway. We get stuck in a rut of maintaining our traditions, processes, or formulas, often not recognizing when they are not working. Many parents and coaches make the mistake of holding on to the reigns of control so long that they miss valuable windows of opportunity to get input and insight from other coaches on how to get better. The baby birds must eventually leave the nest and the cubs have to leave the den. As parents and coaches, we must learn when it is time to let go to grow.

Lesson in the Loss

One of the ways we can get better is to learn a lesson from every loss. Our middle daughter, Jasmine, has a saying: "Winning is fun, and fun is winning". However, we cannot win every game; yet, we can personify grace and honor the game with good sportsmanship despite the loss. In the same respect, we can glean some valuable information from the loss as well. Serena Williams spoke with the wisdom of a great champion when she said:

> *"I've grown most, not from victories, but from setbacks. If winning is God's reward, then losing is how he teaches us."*
> – *Serena Williams*

None of us are perfect. We all make mistakes, and it takes a great deal of emotional intelligence to own up to our mistakes. When we can forgive ourselves and others for our own errors and shortcomings, we form lasting relationships that will stand the test of time. This is very important concept to grasp, especially in the parent-child coaching relationship.

The Art of Constructive Criticism

Delivering criticism is an art form. Most student-athletes have a bit of ego. Egos need to be stroke, but the message still needs to be delivered. You must find ways to deliver the message in a way that is honest but does not necessarily tear them down and ruin their confidence.

We always try to include something positive by making each moment a teachable moment. When talking to our kids, we purposefully have them address the issue so that they can be a part of the solution to make the corrective action. This develops the life skill of learning to accept constructive criticism and critical thinking. For example, if William is having a bad shooting game, we ask him about what about his technique could he analyze to improve his shooting percentage, or what could have helped him stay mentally focused in the game. Once we have identified the problem with William, he is able to see where we are coming and can take corrective action on his own. When people feel that they are a part of the solution, they have a lower tendency to take offense to what is being said.

The strategy of layering negative criticism with some positive feedback and observations is another way to make criticism more digestible. Start with a compliment or some praise, then express the negative point, followed up by applause for something else you noticed the student player did well. Think about it like a peanut butter and jelly sandwich – the peanut butter adheres to the roof of your mouth, but the jelly is so sweet you hardly ever notice the stickiness. It is important to have more positives rather than negative because this allows you to continue to build up your child's self-esteem and confidence in their skill level while still encouraging them to find a way to get better.

The timing of criticism is also important. Perhaps right after the match or right after the game is not the right time to delve into all the things the child did wrong. Unloading all your ideas and insights at the wrong time might just fall on a deaf ear. Sometimes it is better to reserve the discussion until later. Kids also value privacy. No kid wants to be embarrassed in front of their peers or friends or a crowd. Some things are best left said one-on-one or within the coaching team. It is best to be concise and clear with your delivery so that the messages are not lost in translation or buried in a long message.

Another factor to consider when talking to a student athlete is to approach them with a positive tone. Tone is key because the way you say something can be taken in different ways. If a parent yells at their child about not doing something, this might cause the child to become defensive and combative. It is hard to listen when you are angry.

In summary, as a parent, mentor or coach, you want your message to be heard and not tuned out, so you must learn to deliver the message in a way that is received and taken to heart. Our advice to the triple threat student- athlete is to be cognoscente of the qualities that make you a coachable athlete. To get the best results, this process of critically thinking about performance and listening to ways to improve needs to start as early as possible. And that all begins with developing and training a triple threat child to have a strong mindset.

Reading and Listening Exploration

- *The High School Sports Parent – Developing Triple Impact Competitors* by Jim Thompson (Positive Coaching Alliance)
- *Raising Athletic Stars: How to Put Integrity and Character Development Back in Play* by Theodore S. Dance
- *7 Habits of Highly Effective Teens* by Sean R. Covey
- *Emotional Intelligence 2.0 by* Travis Bradberry and Jean Greaves
- *Coach Yourself to Success* by Talane Miedaner
- *See Jane Lead* by Lois P. Frankel

Lesson 8

Train the Mind, Body, Spirit

Contributor: Jasmine Jeffress

"You are never really playing an opponent.
You are playing yourself, your own highest standards,
and when you reach your limits, that is real joy."

– Arthur Ashe

We love the commercial with Stephen Curry that says: Train the mind and the body will follow. This is a mantra that we have strived to follow in sport and in life. Every job or sport requires a set of skills that a person needs to acquire if they want to be the best. There are many people competing for the same positions. Each skill is another advantage that puts a person in front of someone else. The skill people tend to neglect and underestimate the most is the power of the mind. A tough mindset is the difference between being the best and being mediocre. A large majority of people believe that studying and working out is what will get them where they need to go, but that is not true at all. The secret ingredient – the secret sauce – to cataclysmic success is mental toughness.

A strong mentality plays an astounding role when it comes to determining how far a person is willing to go to reach a goal. A weak mentality always gets in the way of fulfilling someone's deepest desires. It takes a lot to be on the top of the winner's box whether that is for school, sports, or a job. It is a mixture of faith, discipline, resilience, and many other things. There are too many people that think things are easier than they are. No one realizes how much work a person must go through to get accomplished what they have accomplished.

Tony Robbins, one of the great motivational speakers in world wrote a book called Awaken the Giant Within that makes a great point: "The three decisions that control your destiny are: 1) Your decisions about what to focus on. 2) Your decisions about what things mean to you. and 3) Your decisions about what to do to create the results you desire".

Faith and **dedication** are two words that everyone should think about when they picture what they want in their future because that faith is the belief in what cannot be seen, and dedication is the habit that will get them there. Sometimes when things get difficult, this is when your mind needs to be strong and rely on your faith and self-discipline to remain dedicated to your craft. Trust the process is a mantra we rely a lot on when talking about staying mentally focused. What this saying means to us is that you must have faith in a certain method of doing things that will ultimately have a positive outcome if you just stay mentally strong and stick to it.

Effort is another factor that is shaped by mental willpower. A person's input will, for the most part, match the output. A person can go to practice for two hours and be great, but a person who goes to practice for 4 hours will be better. One person might read over chapters to study for their exam, but the person who reads the chapters and makes an outline has a better understanding of the material

Developing a relentless **work ethic** goes hand in hand with effort. Someone must decide how much work they are willing to put in to get what they want out of it. They must determine how much their goals are worth it. This is the part where passion and heart come into play. One must first decide what it is that they want. Next, they should decide what they are willing to do to get it.

Our daughter Jasmine decided that she wanted to complete the International Baccalaureate program. This program is not just meant for anyone. It is a program of rigorous courses that challenge one's intellectual skills, mental skills, and ability to find a balance. The program starts in a student's junior year and finishes their senior year. Jasmine's junior year was a lot to take in. At first, she struggled to keep up with these accelerated courses. She had a lot of self-doubt and felt as if she was not smart enough to keep up with the workload. After some time, she realized it was not that she was not smart enough, it was the fact that she was not applying herself to her full potential. When she decided that she was going to dedicate more time to studying, that is when she became the student we always knew her to be. After coming home with grades that were not up to her standards, she decided that it would not happen anymore. Using her resilience and passion, she earned that international baccalaureate diploma. She was so determined to get it, she even found a way to balance it with volleyball and her social life. When she set her mind to it, the sky was the limit. There were many tears and countless meltdowns, but when her mind became committed, her heart followed. Her heart is what gave her that extra push.

There are also many **sacrifices** that a person must make. To be the best you must devote many hours to the craft you are trying to hone. Sometimes it is hard to sacrifice certain things, especially for teenagers. The thought of missing the end of the year party is dreadful but missing a tournament or job opportunity is worse because the second option will help get you closer to your goal.

When it comes to sports, a lot of people train athletically, but their minds are weak. A strong body needs a strong mind. The question is how does one build a stronger mind? The answer – **counseling**. Many professional athletes use a **counselor,** such as coach, a spiritual advisor, therapist, sports psychologist, or psychiatrist, to help teach them certain mental skills that will help improve their performance. Counseling is not just about finding ways to win. Depression, anxiety, and suicide are real issues that need to be addressed. The counseling sessions should focus on skills to cope with stress, maintain composure, build confidence, conquer fear, and visualize feats or goals they want to accomplish. Consulting a therapist, sports psychologist, or psychiatrist is never a sign of weakness, but a mature step in dealing with issues that may be preventing you from moving forward past a plateau on which are you are stuck. It is a valuable resource to help students become more self-aware.

The first step to embracing counseling is to be okay talking and improving our **communication** skills. Building a strong mind must translate into developing a strong voice. We have to build the confidence to be assertive in our personal lives, school lives and our sports lives. We must speak up and talk. Communication is a powerful tool. There is a saying that communication can solve 90 % of problems. Communication must be a two-way street between a parent or mentor and their child, a student and their teacher and/or counselor, a player and their coach. Communication is the bridge that makes sure that everyone is on the same page. It is better to over communicate rather than under communicate because when there is no communication there are holes that lead to big gaps of misunderstandings. Communication can also help make a person feel better because it opens up another way of thinking, eases anxiety, and leads to great knowledge of self.

The next important skill to work on for mental strength is **visualization**. It is important to see yourself accomplishing a thing even before you do it. You must envision a powerful ability in your own being, knowing you can conquer anything you set your mind to achieving.

During the counseling sessions, the athlete can communicate many different feelings, such as if they are feeling fear, if they are feeling pressure of losing or not disappointing a coach or a loved one. Sometimes it is the fear of failure or performing in front of big crowds. Whatever the fear, whatever the issue, student-athletes can learn strategies how allow their fear fuel them, instead of fueling their own fears. Then they become an overcomer and learn to mentally push past artificial limits that they put on their minds.

Along the lines of visualization, another habit that helps us shine in the big moments is the power of affirmation and meditation. An **affirmation** is "an act or an instance of affirming - declaring an action that you would like to see take place".

Affirmations are critical to developing mental strength. They are just as important as physically practicing buzzer beaters, sudden death overtime shootouts, two-minute drills, or that uber-important recital or audition dance routine. Affirmations can be in the form of poems or prayers that feed our spirit, and music or lyrics that soothe our soul. They help us meditate on good thoughts that we know to be true about ourselves. Affirmations are instrumental in maintaining a sound proof room when we need to drown out negative thoughts or quiet the rowdy crowd in our head that heckles us. Affirmations tip the balance to outweigh out negative thoughts from the self-sabotage that easily derails us. So, given these powerful uses of affirmations, we must remember to recite and meditate on them daily if you want to prepare for the big stages and the big moments in life. One of my favorite affirmations to recite every day is a powerful poem by Lisa Nichols. Recite it with me:

I AM ENOUGH!

"I stand here
In my greatness.
I own my light.
I own my brilliance.
I am bold.
I am courageous.
I am perfect
in my perfection.
This is my time!
This is my time!
I'm bright enough.
I'm old enough.
I've experienced enough.
I'm wise enough.
I understand that
I. Am. Enough."

In summary, mental strength is as important as physical strength, and being grounded spiritually can elevate you to a whole other level. By following these simple tips, you can push past fear and take the limits off your mind. It requires faith, dedication, effort, work ethic, counseling, communication, visualization, meditation, and affirmation. If there is any doubt in this recipe, just remember the mantra – "Train the mind, and the body will follow."

Reading and Listening Exploration

Mental Strength:

- *Abundance Now: Amplify Your Life and Achieve Prosperity Today* by Janet Switzer and Lisa Nichols
- *Super Nevaeh: Daily Affirmations for Children* by Nevaeh McCauley
- *Reprogram Your Mindset: 100 Winning Quotes and Affirmations for High Performers* by Toni A. Haley, MD
- *Positive Athlete Affirmations Audible Audio Book* by Stephen Hyang and narrated by Dan McGowan
- *Thrive: The Third Metric to Redefining Success and Creating a Life of Well-Being, Wisdom, and Wonder* by Arianna Huffington
- *Stretch to Win* by Ann Frederick and Chris Frederick
- *The Best of Les Brown Audio Collection: Inspiration from the World's Leading Motivational Speaker* by Les Brown

Wellness, Nutrition and Fitness:

- *The Fitness Mindset: Eat for Energy, Train for Tension, Manage Your Mindset, Reap the Results* by Brian Keane
- *PUSH: 30 days to Turbocharged Habits, Bangin' Body and the Life You Deserve* by Chalene Johnson

- *Complete Food and Nutrition Guide* published by the Academy of Nutrition and Dietetics
- *Fitness Nutrition: The Ultimate Fitness Guide* by Nicholas Bjorn
- *Run Fast, Eat Slow: Nourishing Recipes for Athletes* by Shalane Flanagan and Elise Kopecky
- *Strength Training Bible for Women* by David Kirschen & William Smith, Foreword: Julia Ladewski
- *Bigger, Leaner, Stronger: The Simple Science of Building the Ultimate Male Body* by Michael Matthews
- *15 Minute Meals to Your Pain Freedom* by Dr. Zarinah Hud, DO
- *50 Holistic Treatments for Kids 5 and Under* by Dr. Pam Middleton, MD

Spiritual Nourishment:

- *SOAR: Build Your Vision from the Ground Up!* by T.D. Jakes
- *The Alchemist* by Paulo Coelho
- *I Am Number 8* by John Gray
- *The Case for Christ: A Journalist's Personal Investigation of the Evidence for Jesus* by Lee Strobel (also a movie)
- *The Big Deal of Taking Small Steps Closer to God* by Vashti Murphy McKenzie
- *The Purpose Driven Life* by Rick Warren
- *Better Your Day By What You Think and Say: 21 Audio Devotionals* by Joyce Meyer

Lesson 9

Be in Service to Others

Contributors: William Jeffress, Jr.

*"Everybody can be great...because anybody can serve.
You don't have to have a college degree to serve.
You don't have to make your subject and verb agree to serve.
You only need a heart full of grace. A soul generated by love."*

-Martin Luther King, Jr.

Ⓦe do not want student-athletes to just be good, we want them to do good in the world. Many people associate athletics with excellence and accolades. However, strength of character, integrity, generosity, caring for others more than you care for yourself, and the ability to show gratitude are all noble qualities that any good student-athlete should want to develop. It is admirable that many amateur student-athletes and professional athletes mobilize their platforms to participate in service projects.

In our house we follow the organizational motto of our children's God Mother:

"Meeting needs and solving problems for the benefit of all humanity."

– Dr. Metashar Dillon, CEO
Kingdom International Economic Development Corporation and
T.I.G.R.E. One Million Dollar Women's Global Entrepreneur Competition

They usually choose a charity in their community to help based on that organization providing a solution to a problem that is close to their heart. This gives them more reason to look forward to helping others. It is important to pick a project or a cause that the person is passionate about. Of course, if you enjoy the work then it is fun and is more of an honor than a chore. Many athletes, such as LeBron James and Kevin Durant, choose to give back to their hometowns and other places in the U.S. that hold special places in their hearts. Kevin Durant, the sponsor of William's elite travel basketball team, made us so proud when he won the Most Valuable Player of the NBA Finals and the 2017-18 NBA Cares Community Assist Award for his outstanding charitable and philanthropic efforts. These two star players are prime examples of men leaving behind community action legacies that will live on long beyond their play in sport.

More important than recognition and awards, an athlete who volunteers gleans valuable life skills through the learning that takes place during the volunteering. This is called **"Service Learning"**. According to Vanderbilt University's Janet S. Eyler (winner of the 2003 Thomas Ehrlich Faculty Award for Service Learning) and Dwight E. Giles, Jr., service learning is outlined by the following definition: "a form of experiential education where learning occurs through a cycle of action and reflection as students seek to achieve real objectives for the community and deeper understanding and skills for themselves. In the process, students link personal and social development with academic and cognitive development; experience enhances understanding; understanding leads to more effective action."

There are many benefits to service learning and community engagement. Being of service to others has a positive impact on their academic and cognitive knowledge skill set. It also can improve their ability to always apply what they are learning in the real world. It helps them use critical thinking to learn how to problem solve and analyze real world problems. These are all amazing qualities that will help a person as they grow older. Learning something this valuable early in life can save someone from mistakes that can be avoided. Instilling the behavior of service to others will help people find the value and discipline to continue it on as they grow.

According to Cathryn Berger Kaye, M.A., author of *The Complete Guide to Service Learning: Proven, Practical Ways to Engage Students in Civic Responsibility, Academic Curriculum, Social Action*, several criteria are the hallmarks of service learning:

- Academic relevance, rigor, and application
- Social analysis and high-level thinking
- Youth initiative, voice and choice
- Aspects of social and emotional integration
- Inquiry
- Observing change over time
- Purpose and process
- Emphasis of intrinsic over extrinsic
- Reciprocal partnership
- Career ideas

- Global Connections
- Literature integration
- Reflection

In our family, volunteer work is a regular occurrence. We both sit on a few civic boards. Adrianna has volunteered through her NCAA College tennis team feeding patrons at the soup kitchen for 4 years. Jasmine needed volunteer hours for volleyball team and international baccalaureate program. She did her service hours at a nursing home and the YMCA. William had to have volunteer hours to be admitted to and remain enrolled in the McDowell High School honors college. They all learned many lessons from the different places at which they volunteered. Through volunteering it opened their eyes to the fact that even simple work can help someone go a long way. This passage is submitted in the spring of 2018 by our son, William Jeffress, Jr. about his volunteer service learning experience:

"My volunteer hours were done at the Booker T. Washington Center, as well as the Erie Rise Leadership Academy Charter School in city of Erie, PA. I tutored math and English vocabulary. I also helped organize and play games that demonstrated teamwork and leadership and had an impact on kids' lives that I believe will last a lifetime.

Throughout my service hours, the most difficult days were the first ones. This is because I had to get used to the environment and the kids. I felt nervous and anxious to start my work. After adjusting and getting over my mental fears, I felt free to assist the children. I started off by playing games with them after lunch. I helped them learn how to play, how to have respect for other players, and be fair.

I never thought that community service could make me feel differently about myself, but it has. It has made me feel better because I know what I can do to influence the world. That a little bit of my time can have a big impact on the lives around me. I feel as though life is not just for living. It is for touching others and putting smiles on faces you are not so familiar with. If you make others happy, you in turn are happier too.

Some things I have learned from this experience is that teaching and directing is harder than it looks. Kids learn at different paces. Some need to be sped up and others slowed down. Without one on one attention with some kids, they will not understand the topic being taught. It is not that they are unintelligent, it is that they have not been directed enough to fully grasp the concept. They must be guided in the right direction by a helping hand.

In conclusion, volunteering was overall a great experience. It allowed me to learn new things, experience more of life, meet new people, and see another side of myself that has never been shown. Working with kids is something I now appreciate and enjoy. It allows me to connect to them and see new perspectives. This is something I would like to continue to do in my life. A little time and effort can mean more than you think to one person or a whole organization."

If you have not volunteered, we encourage you to do so. Volunteer work also helps to build character in a person. Students can get a greater sense of personal growth on a moral and spiritual level. It helps some with the leadership skills because they learn to use their interpersonal skills to improve their communication. This will help build a strong foundation for when they need to communicate with many different types of people.

Volunteering also helps students learn real world business skills, such as event management, communication, accounting, graphic design, business marketing, administrative duties, and networking to name a few. The network and community connections are very important because these are the people who will support, and you get to know other people that can help get you to the end goal. All these factors help improve their self-development, self-awareness, and self-identity. It can also help their confidence which will translate to leadership in their sport arena.

> *"Service combined with learning adds value to each and transforms both."* – *Honnet and Poulsen*

The take home message is that to be celebrated in school and idolized in sports is an amazing feeling, but it cannot compare to the feeling you get when you do good in the world. As Zig Ziglar, once said, "If you go our looking for friends, you're going to find they are very scarce. If you go out to be a friend, you'll find them everywhere". The key message we want all young people to know – athlete or not – is summed up in this single sentence:

> *"We make a living by what we get, but we make a life by what we give."* – *Winston Churchill*

So, take our advice…

- Have a spirit of gratitude
- Give back and learn
- Be a good friend to someone in need, and
- Be in service to others.

…because it is always a blessing to be a blessing to someone else.

Reading and Listening Exploration

- *The Complete Guide to Service Learning: Proven, Practical Ways to Engage Students in Civic Responsibility, Academic Curriculum, Social Action* by Cathryn Berger Kaye
- *Volunteer with Your Kids* article by Jenny Friedman-Parents Magazine
- *The Cathedral Within: Transforming Your Life by Giving Something Back* by Bill Shore
- *Pass the Mustard Seed: It's Your Faith that Moves Mountains, Not Our Hands* by Desiree Lee
- *Life Wisdom: Inspire to be Great* - Quotes by Zig Ziglar
- *Love Does* by Bob Goff

Lesson 10

Knowledge is Key

"If knowledge is the key and mentoring and coaching are the doors, you can unlock your future and walk through them."

– Andrea Jeffress

Knowledge is key. We all say, "if I knew what I knew today when I was much younger, I would be so much further ahead." Through our experiences, we have learned that the most efficient way to start your journey is to have someone show you the way. Getting a good coach or mentor is like taking a flight to California rather than driving in a car across the country. That is why we are fully invested in the mentoring process. Having the right mentor can reduce your learning curve tenfold. The earlier you start your mentoring relationship the better the outcomes will be. If knowledge is the key and mentoring and coaching are the doors, you can unlock your future and walk through them.

Reading is Fundamental

There is a book we have both read and found motivating – "Think and Grow Rich" by Napoleon Hill and Dennis Kimbro – but if we had to write a book, it would be called "Read and Be Mentored". In our opinion, reading is fundamental, and both coaching and mentoring put you on the fast track to knowledge.

> "If you want to get ahead, then you must become knowledgeable about where you're going. If you know where you are going, then it is only natural to want to get ahead. Once you are knowledgeable about the path you have chosen, you're ready to begin your journey."

> – William S. Jeffress

Knowledge, wisdom and guidance from a parent, coach or mentor can take you to where you want to go faster than you can go alone. That was one of the main reasons for creating the book and the SMART JOCKS College and Career Readiness Portal through an online subscription resource center available through the website at **www.smartjocks.com**.

Our first goal of this book and resource portal is to encourage you to read. The rates of illiteracy are alarming in our nation and are directly tied to lower wage earnings and higher prison rates. We have to break the cycle of the school to prison pipeline by attacking the problem of illiteracy in our young people. With video games and social media, it is hard to get kids and adults alike to put down their devices and read (unless it's an electronic book on a device of course). People have to be encouraged to read to unlock their imagination and journey into a world of new opportunities. Kids are more likely to read if they see adults around them reading.

Mentoring, Coaching and Recruitment

Besides gaining knowledge through reading, student-athletes also gain knowledge from being coached and mentored. The adults in their circle who have volunteered to be coaches and mentors are partners in their success. They help student-athletes become more self-aware and provide you access to lessons to acquire new skills, give you feedback on your skill development and open doors of opportunity to be recruited to higher levels in sports and career as well.

Becoming an elite student-athlete can put you in a situation where you are constantly being recruited. The recruitment process starts as early as primary schools, collegiate institutions, and continues into the professional and corporate world. Being knowledgeable of the recruitment process can put you on the fast track for success.

Knowing the recruitment process is important because it is the process of finding the best-qualified candidate – within or outside of an organization. The process is often performed in a timely and cost-effective manner. Recruiting includes analyzing the requirements of an opening or position, attracting participants to that opening, screening and selecting applicants, and finally integrating the new recruit to the organization and acclimating them to the position.

Most people do not understand that this process involves finding the right fit. When it comes to schools and colleges, it makes perfect sense to embed yourself in the recruitment process as a potential applicant. It is also the applicant's job to evaluate the potential organization just as much as organization is evaluating them. One must research the organizations faculty, academic and coaching staff, teammates, facilities, location, cost, and other amenities. This knowledge is key in order to find the right fit.

Self-Assessment

It is also key for all of the team members to be knowledgeable about each other and especially the student athlete. The parent, mentor, coach and student-athlete should all complete a personality test and a strengths, weaknesses, opportunities, and threats (SWOT) analysis together. During William's participation in the 2018 Nike Elite Top 100 camp, this concept was presented to the players by Dr. Ramel L. Smith, PhD, as a "SCOT" analysis - strengths, challenges, opportunities, and threats. Figuring out personality type and doing a SWOT/SCOT analysis raises self-awareness and really helps a person get to know themselves better, discover ways to improve quickly based on their gifts and gain insight to attack challenges and threats. Regardless of which self-assessment system you adopt, the critical analysis will give you a stepping stone to assist you in setting goals and figuring out interventions to make to changes to improve.

SWOT analysis

- Strengths
- Weaknesses
- Opportunities
- Threats

SCOT analysis

- Strengths
- Challenges
- Opportunities
- Threats

For the purposes of this book, we will use the SWOT method. The most important part of the SWOT analysis is to form connections between the strengths and opportunities while also figuring out which weaknesses and threats need to be examined, evaluated, and strengthened. In the end, SWOT can be used to cater to multiple scenarios and can be very useful when preparing for academic or athletic success to get recruited. Here are examples of our kids' past SWOT analyses:

Adrianna's SWOT Analysis: Tennis

STRENGTHS

- Academically sound with both parents actively involved and college educated. An avid reader. Ability to succeed in a large academic setting. Exceptional leader. Independent. Disciplined.
- Parents familiar with academic and athletic process.
- Very athletic with good size and height.
- Ability to compete athletically on an elite level.
- Has a desire to succeed both academically and athletically.
- Strong public school system
- Dedicated Primary Coaches

WEAKNESSES

- Limted desire to partner with classmates to partner with on an academic level.
- Minimal teammates to partner with to challenge on an athletic level.
- Does not interact socially with friends with similar goals.
- Local teams not very strong.
- Needs to imporve strength physically and mentally.
- Minimal athletic role models to follow at the high school level.

OPPORTUNITIES

- With tutoring should be able to move into honors program.
- With the proper training could be an elite player.
- Has the ability to particpate in several different sports.
- Has the resources to train and travel.
- Local access to facilities.
- Open minded to academic and athletic pathways.

THREATS

- Limited summer youth education programs and family support.
- Geographically isolated with minimal elite tennis training programs and travel > 2 hours required.
- Inclement weather makes it difficult to play outside year round.
- The bad weather during the academic year limits travel.
- Does not like video instruction or post match analysis.
- Preferred not to have parent coach as primary in later years.

Jasmine's SWOT Analysis: Volleyball

STRENGTHS
- Academically strong with both parents actively involved and college educated. An avid reader. Ability to succeed in a large academic setting.
- Very social and has a large number of friends.
- Exceptional leader. Contagious humor. Disciplined.
- Parents familiar with academic and athletic process.
- Very athletic with limited size and height.
- Ability to compete athletically on an elite level.
- Has a desire to succeed academically.
- Strong private school system.

WEAKNESSES
- Prone to injury.
- Struggles with time-management needed for academic success.
- Needs to improve strength.
- No motivation to seek outside help when challenged academically.
- Had no desire to be an elite athlete but enjoys team atmosphere and being around friends.

OPPORTUNITIES
- With the proper training could be an elite student.
- Has the ability to particpate in several different sports.
- Has the resources to train and travel.
- Access to summer education programs worldwide.
- Open minded to academic and athletic pathways.

THREATS
- Distracted by social activities.
- Limited access to programs or trainers in the area to develop an elite student.
- Isolated location in northwestern PA.
- The bad weather during the academic year limits travel.
- No parental involvement in terms of parental coaching.

William's SWOT Analysis: Basketball

STRENGTHS

- Academically strong at gifted level with both parents actively involved and college educated. Ability to succeed in a large academic setting.
- Identifiable classmates to partner with to challenge on an academic level. Very social and has a core group of friends.
- Exceptional leader. Meticulous nature. Solid work ethic.
- Very athletic with exceptional size and height. Fast and agile for height.
- Ability to compete athletically on an elite level.
- Other parents in the area with similar goals for their children.
- Has a desire to succeed both academically and athletically.

WEAKNESSES

- Dislikes reading outside of school assignments.
- Local high school not on national level.
- No local travel teams on national circuit.
- Needs to improve strength physically.
- Needs to work on creativity.
- Needs to works mental strength.
- Struggles with managing time and assignments.
- No current athletic role models to follow at the high school level.

OPPORTUNITIES

- Ability to take AP courses for future college credit
- With the proper training could be an elite player.
- Has the resources to train and travel.
- Local access to facilities.
- Open minded to academic and athletic pathways.

THREATS

- Limited summer youth education programs.
- Isolated location in northwestern PA.
- The bad weather during the academic year in order to travel.
- Distraction from goals due to other people and activities.

In summary, a parent, mentor, coach and student-athlete should all complete a personality survey and the SWOT/SCOT analysis together. The self-assessment profiles are useful, but in-person testing or getting the self-assessment results interpreted by a certified testing administrator or trained Sports Psychologist/Psychiatrist specializing is ideal. After doing personality testing and the SWOT/SCOT analysis, then you can sit down with the student athlete and discuss an action plan to address each of the four categories. This analysis will also help to plan to acquire the correct team members and resources needed to accomplish your goals if they not already a part of the team. From there you can come up with mutually agreed upon objectives between the athlete, parent, mentor, coach and the team. This will help you further develop the learning action plan that will guide your schedule of training events and interventions (both athletic and academic). No learning action plan should be complete without writing, journaling and reading – audio or visual – whatever the learning method – just get it done.

"Today knowledge has power.

It controls access to opportunity and advancement."

– Peter F. Drucker

If you approach life using these pearls of wisdom – read for knowledge, analyze and become knowledgeable about oneself, work hard to secure excellent mentoring and coaching to get on the fast track and get ahead – you will ultimately become a top recruit and #1 draft pick on and off the court.

Reading and Listening Exploration

- *Failing Up: How to Take Risks, Aim Higher, and Never Stop Learning* by Leslie Odom, Jr.
- *Wired That Way-A Comprehensive Guide to Understanding and Maximizing Your Personality Type* by Marita Littauer
- *If Only We Knew What We Know* by Carla O'Dell, C. Jackson Grayson, Jr. with Wily Essaides
- *Webinar: The CASPer Assessment Test [a research-based, online, video-scenario based, situational judgement test (SJT) which more than 70000 students have taken since 2010.]* Developed by Dr. Harold Reiter and Dr. Kelly Dore; https://takecasper.com/casper-information-webinar-june-1-2018/
- Personality Assessment Questionnaire Resources – Examples: Myers Briggs Personality Test Indicator (MBTI) and Guilford Zimmerman Temperament Survey. Note: self-assessment profiles are useful, but in-person testing or getting the self-assessment results interpreted by a certified testing administrator or trained Sports Psychologist/Psychiatrist specializing is ideal.
- *The New Edge in Knowledge Management is Changing the Way We Do Business* by Carla O'dell and Cindy Hubert

Bonus: Lesson 11

The Backup Plan:

Don't Go Back, Go Forward

"You are never too old to set another goal or to dream a new dream."

-C.S. Lewis

We all need to think beyond the dream and beyond the game by establishing a contingency back-up plan. Some people agree with celebrities like Elizabeth Holmes who said, "I think the minute that you have a backup plan, you've admitted that you're not going to succeed" or like Malorie Blackman who said, "A back up plan means somewhere in my head, I think I might fail and that word is not in my vocabulary. Plus, I'm too talented to fail."

However, in the case of elite level student-athletes, we know that NCAA statistics say less than 1% of players are going to make it to the pros and only a small percentage of high school athletes, 3-6%, are going to go on to make it to the college team rosters; even if they do, only about 2% of college athletes earn a full-ride college scholarship.

Certainly, having a backup plan does not mean foregoing your dream at all because you are unsure or because it may be difficult. It certainly does not admit or suggest weakness or failure. As Bob Goff, founder of Restore International and author of the New York Times Best Seller, "Love Does", shared his wisdom: "Don't let uncertainty talk you into pursuing a backup plan instead of your purpose". However, realistically we should recognize the need to develop a plan to transition back to society as an employee or entrepreneur, using our business and vocational skills and pursuing whatever our passion may be. Ideally, everyone needs a plan if the dream falls short, in case of catastrophic injury, or when the amateur or professional career has ended. **In essence, the backup plan is really the forward plan that keeps your life moving in a positive direction after your active participation in sports ends.**

Making a back-up plan can be accomplished by broadening our scopes of interest and pursuing other passions, hobbies, and disciplines outside of the sports arena. This underscores the importance of focusing on academics, learning valuable trade skills, developing entrepreneurial ideas, polishing business skills, and networking. Athletes with outlets and contingency plans have less rates of depression, anxiety and suicide, and that fact alone should encourage us to find a way to build a life after sport where we continue to build success.

We have all run into situations when our ideal plan gets derailed and does not become fulfilled. If you're a skeptic and non-believer that it can happen to you, check out former basketball standout and my self-publishing consultant guru's book – "Inmate 1142980: The Desiree Lee Story" – which is now a documentary and movie. Another good example on this subject is that a student athlete could enroll in college majoring in engineering and realize that the program is not a good fit for them. It is always good to have a backup plan or a safety net to still achieve a successful outcome without missing a beat. It is also good to make sure your academic curriculum program has rigor and is not a useless or "empty" degree with little practical value. When you finish school, you should possess a degree that can open doors for you.

When you finish higher level education, you may consider entering graduate school to get a master's degree or a terminal doctoral degree. If you are going to take this route, you need to see your counselors of class advisors to get on tract to study for the graduate admission tests (GRE's, GMATs, MCAT, LSAT) and make sure you have all the curricular pre-requisites to apply.

An education is important because your sports career will end. Then what? Your ability to create a life after sports is critical for children and your children's children. It's about the legacy you will leave of the earth for generations to come.

One famed football star that is making business moves is Tamba Hali, famed Kansas City Chiefs pass rusher and native son of Liberia, Africa. He has played 12 years in NFL and is finding his passion and purpose in teaching future NFL and college stars the pearls of football. He is also pursuing a career in music and giving back to his native country of Liberia.

Heinz Ward is another football great pursuing business and furthering his mission by traveling the country as a keynote speaker and giving back through his foundation called "Helping Hands Foundation", which champions inner city and underprivileged children in Pittsburgh and has given over $100,000 in college scholarships.

Jamal Mashburn is another excellent example of a superb athlete thriving in business well beyond the court. After playing for Kentucky in college and then three NBA teams, he is now retired. When he was younger, he said his Mom told him to stay in the books and computers in case basketball did not work out. He never imagined playing into his late 30's-40's and traded in his ball for a brief case, like the one he always saw the men at the metro train stations carrying. True to his dreams, he was very wise with his money and made smart investments that built an impressive business empire, leaving a legacy for generations to come. He owned more than 80 franchise locations and five car dealerships, including 40 Papa John's locations, 38 Outback Steakhouse restaurants, and 4 Dunkin' Donuts. In 2013, he partnered with former NFL player, Winston Justice, to launch a venture capital firm for investing in high-tech startups called Mashburn Justice Capital Partners. In 2014, Mashburn also launched a marketing agency, Mashburn Sackett, with branches in Chicago and Miami, which serve the growing interest in smaller agencies that respond with greater agility to internet changes. The firm specializes in interactive, experiential, and viral marketing, social media, integrated film and 3D production, among other related digital services (Source: Black Entrepreneur Online Magazine). He believes your back up plan "is almost like not falling back on something but falling forward to something."

When Magic Johnson retired from basketball after announcing he had contracted the HIV virus, he launched a backup plan that had a rival of no other. Through his many business mentors, he established valuable relationships with over the course of his career. He took the business lessons he had learned very seriously and turned lemons onto lemonade, amassing a fortune through a conglomerate of businesses providing he and his family with multiple revenue streams. These were businesses such as Starbucks Franchise, the Los Angeles Dodgers Baseball owners group, TV Commentating and Journalism, and movie entertainment complexes all around the United States to name a few.

We are all familiar with Michael Jordan, Shaquille and Tiger Woods and their billionaire status achieved by more than their abilities on the court and the golf course. Their equipment and apparel businesses and entertainment pursuits such as movies and music that anchor their colossal brand empires.

But what about those athletes doing the most beyond the world of sports? Did you know that LeBron James is an author who has channeled his creative genius and imagination to dabble in writing non-fiction and fiction stories his whole life? Yes! He has had several books published, including a book series named "Sam Hain – Occult Detective" penned under his author name Bron James. He has also executive produced a TV show about entrepreneurs in Cleveland called the Cleveland Hustle. He and his wife, Savannah, are also philanthropists who are building up the Akron Community and greater Cleveland community through the LeBron James Family Foundation.

Speaking of families, sisters, Venus Williams and Serena Williams, are our idols for more than the legends they have become on the tennis court. When the naysayers were critical of them for deviating from tennis to focus on going back to school to start businesses and complete their education and for vocational training in the fashion, nail and music industry, they did it anyway. Now they are the creative architects of monstrously successful fashion lines, businesses, and production houses. They also made some savvy legacy business moves and became part owners of an NFL team, the Miami Dolphins. These legendary sisters and extraordinary gentlemen are some of our proudest examples of triple threat athletes who demonstrate the importance of using education, network mentoring, and vocational training to develop a viable back up plan that will guarantee that they live a prosperous and fulfilling life beyond the world of sports.

And we can do the same. Whatever your dream, follow your passion and find your purpose. Don't go back, go forward. Formulate a plan, make it your own, and live it well.

All you have to do is... dream.

"The most important thing to remember is this: to be ready at any moment to give up what you are for what you might become."

– W.E.B. DuBois

Reading and Listening Exploration

- NextLevelLeadershipBlog.com by Mr. Chad Shapiro and Mr. Marwan Powell
- *The Purpose Driven Life* by Rick Warren
- *Voices of Inspiration: Real Life Wisdom for Living Your Best Life* by Marlon Smith
- *Wellness Your Way: The Short and Sweet Guide to Creating Your Custom Plan for a Happier, Healthier Life* by Dr. Donna L. Hamilton, MD
- Travelpedia: A Quick Guide on How to Travel Efficiently, Healthy, and Safely by Dr. Yvette McQueen, MD
- *Resist* by Veronica Chambers (pre-release 9/2018)
- *White Paper Magic* by Andrea Jeffress (pre-release)
- *Be the Plan* by Andrea Jeffress (pre-release)
- *Released – The Movie – and the book Inmate 1142980: The Desiree Lee Story* by Desiree Lee
- *On Becoming: Pearls of Wisdom from My Journey into Womanhood* by Dr. Leslie-Ann Williams

FINAL THOUGHTS

"Because all men are created equal, ability is what you make it. It is our education and desire to succeed that distinguishes the man who gets from the man who wants."

- William S. Jeffress

Sports can be used to teach young people to recognize and realize their full potential in life. Sports can help kids stay on the right path. Sports is motivating to students who may be struggling in school to become more focused and study harder to maintain their eligibility for sports. Parents, mentors, teachers and guidance counselors, coaches, administrators, and trainers can all be involved in pushing the student to excel both on and off the field. There may be kids who have higher intelligence, better talent, or more resources more financial resources, but it is the kid who works the hardest who likely succeed.

This book was written primarily for student athletes, parents, coaches, and administrators who would like to be a part of a winning team that ultimately produces an outstanding student-athlete. While it is nearly impossible to completely take the body of knowledge that encompasses all that defines success into one book, SMART JOCKS is merely a foundational resource that addresses the need to have guidance for developing amateur and professional level skills in student athletes at a young age coupled with an ethical obligation to provide our student athletes with a sound intellectual foundation for competing at a high level in life after their sports career is over.

Reading this book will not make you the greatest player, coach, parent or administrator. As in learning any new skill, it takes a lot of practice, repetition and self-discipline. You will learn that being immersed into the exciting and challenging world of sport, academics, and amateur and professional competition is a labor of love and requires a life-long commitment to excellence.

In the end, you will have gained better insight into all the things you have been doing right all along, but you will also be able to identify how to invest in yourself, your child, or your team. You will also learn to recognize the potential pitfalls that you can avoid. Finally, you must take control and evaluate every step you take along this journey. The key is to forge a path, make a plan and have the discipline to stick to it. Your legacy and your future depend on it.

For the student, we leave you will this parting wisdom: Invest in yourself. Play hard and study harder. Your dreams await you, Smart Jock.

ABOUT THE AUTHORS

Andrea Jeffress, MD

Growing up in the inner city and leaving high school to enter college at the age of 14, Dr. Andrea Jeffress knows what it means to have a hand up and not a hand out. Winner of the first scholarship given for the Miss Black Connecticut Scholarship Pageant in 1991, she applied her first of many scholarships to earn her medical degree from the Yale University School of Medicine. Following medical school, she completed her OB/GYN residency at Yale New Haven Hospital. She is now board certified by the American Board of Obstetrics and Gynecology and is a Fellow of the American College of Obstetrics and Gynecology. Dr. Jeffress has been in practice with OB/GYN Associates of Erie, PA since 2000 where she practices general obstetrics and gynecology with an interest in advanced minimally invasive surgical techniques, such as traditional laparoscopy and DaVinci robotic-assisted surgery.

She has many passions and hobbies, including writing, singing, sports, traveling, movies, and the arts; however, her greatest joy is philanthropy and volunteering for civic organizations, such as the Mercyhurst University, the Greater Pennsylvania Alzheimer's Association, the International Trade Forum, True Praise Gospel Group, The Booker T. Washington Center-Mercyhurst Campus, Delta Sigma Theta Sorority, Inc., the 1 Million Dollar Women's Global Entrepreneur Competition, Conference & World Tour, and the Kingdom International Economic Development Corporation. She was recently tapped as the first woman of color appointed to the advisory board of Erie Bank.

Besides medicine, she is an author and copy editor, entrepreneur and small business owner, distributing RAINEATER Wiper Blades (voted best wiper blade by consumers!), Zenedge Energy Drinks, and SMART JOCKS, LLC. She is also a contributing author and editor in the book "Women All Over the World - It's Your Time: Unleashing the Untapped Reservoir of Entrepreneurship Inside Women Worth Trillions of Dollars". She now excited to pursue her passion as the author of her own titles: "White Paper Magic" and "Be the Plan". Her message serves to motivate parents and youth to focus on using higher education, sports and business to build a plan for a brighter future.

Dr. Jeffress is married to William S. Jeffress, and they have three children (Adrianna, Jasmine, and William Jr.). The Jeffresses also raised their nephew, Terrance, and niece, Juanita, and have hosted an exchange student from Nigeria named Olanrewaju Joseph Olamuyiwa. She is co-author of the book and its supplemental workbook and planner: "SMART JOCKS - 10 Lessons Along Our Journey to Raise #1 Draft Picks On and Off the Court".

Dr. William Jeffress

Dr. William Jeffress' mission in life is to motivate youth and adults to harness the power of sport and business to create a better life. Currently, he is the Sport Business Management Program Director and faculty member in the Walker College of Business and Management at Mercyhurst University. He completed course work and was ABD towards a PhD in Organizational Learning and Leadership. He has been conferred an honorary Doctor of Divinity from the Heart Bible Institute for acts of humanitarian service. He received his M.B.A. in Management and Organization and a B.S. in Business Administration from the University of New Haven.

A member of the University of New Haven's Men's Basketball team and a four-year starter, he scored over 1000 points and earned many athletic honors, such as a spot in the Athletic Hall of Fame. After graduation, he was drafted by the United States Basketball League. Unfortunately, he sustained a back injury, which ended his athletic career as a player and catapulted him into the coaching ranks as an assistant coach and head coach for the Amateur Athletic Union, National Intercollegiate Athletic Association, and National Collegiate Athletic Association institutions. After coaching, he became an administrator and faculty member for several colleges and universities in the state of Connecticut, including Quinebaug Valley Community College, University of New Haven, Teikyo-Post University, Gateway Community College, and Yale. He relocated to

Erie and became the Director of Human Resources at Community Health Net, the Executive Director of the Booker T. Washington Center, and now his current position in the Walker College of Business and Management at Mercyhurst University.

Over the years, Dr. Jeffress has held many leadership roles as part of numerous nonprofit organizations to assist the Erie community in addressing healthcare, mental health, education, crime, housing, and youth athletics. Dr. Jeffress is married to Andrea Jeffress, MD, and they have three children (Adrianna, Jasmine, and William Jr.). The Jeffresses also raised their nephew, Terrance, and niece, Juanita, and have hosted an exchange student from Nigeria named Olanrewaju Joseph Olamuyiwa. He is co-author of the book and its supplemental workbook and planner: "SMART JOCKS - 10 Lessons Along Our Journey to Raise #1 Draft Picks On and Off the Court".

Just in time for back to school!

The SMART JOCKS Tool Kit

BE ON TOP OF YOUR GAME WITH A

SMART JOCKS TOOL KIT!

- ✓ **SMART JOCKS Book**
- ✓ **SMART JOCKS Workbook and Planner**
- ✓ **SMART JOCKS College and Career Readiness Portal Membership Subscription**
- ✓ **Free SMART JOCKS MVP Social Media Community Membership**
- ✓ **Free Access to Select Webinars**

The Workbook & Planner Amazon Release Date is 8/8/18. Reserve your autographed copies of the book and workbook and planner via the website today.

The SMART JOCKS College and Career Readiness Portal curriculum launch date begins with each new school year, starting on 9/1/18.

Email: info@smartjocks.com for quotes for bulk purchases.

SMART JOCKS
Membership Subscription
College and Career Readiness
Portal & App

The mission of **SMART JOCKS** is to guide students, adults, and organizations is to harness the power of academics, sport and business to achieve monumental success. We focus on servicing the following areas:

<u>SMART</u>	<u>JOCKS</u>
• Sports & STEM	• Jobs
• Management, Marketing, Mentoring	• Opportunities & Organizations
• Academic & Athletic Advising	• College & Career Advising and Consulting
• Recruitment, Retention & Research	• Kickstarting Knowledge
• Training & Technology	• Service to the Community

Knowledge, wisdom and guidance from a parent, coach or mentor can take you to where you want to go faster than you can go alone. That was the main reason for creating the SMART JOCKS book, the SMART JOCKS Workbook & Planner, and the SMART JOCKS College & Career Readiness Portal and App.

Through our on line courses, mentoring videos, workshops, and webinars and through our personal coaching and sport management, marketing and consulting services, we help student athletes, their support team, professionals and organizations keep their eye on the goal.

How does a membership subscription work for the SMART JOCKS College and Career Readiness Portal?

All you have to do is **SUBSCRIBE** to get started!

Students and the designated support team members (one parent or guardian and one coach) are given weekly assignments throughout the entire academic school year, starting every September through May and have the option for continuing their package during the summer months of June to August.

Through the SMART JOCKS College and Career Readiness Portal and App, we will deliver invaluable content and programming to engage subscribers around the world. SMART JOCKS subscribers (students, parents/guardians, mentors, coaches and school administrators) will have access to a treasure trove of video content tailored by grade level from Kindergarten all the way to 12th grade and beyond, including those headed to post-secondary level education or vocational training.

On the cutting edge, the SMART JOCKS College and Career Readiness Portal and App are designed to harness audio-visual and interactive technology to increase the student's, parent's and mentor's knowledge of the academic and athletic requirements to reach the next level. Even more exciting is that the curriculum will spark college readiness and career exploration through its valuable online resources - new standard in education that should be met for every student across the globe.

The portal is compliant with the American Disabilities Act and provides closed caption technology for the hearing impaired and full audio for the visually impaired.

How do I become a SMART JOCKS subscription member?

To **SUBSCRIBE** to the SMART JOCKS College and Career Readiness Portal and App, go to **www.smartjocks.com** to register yourself, your child, mentee, organization, team, school or school district to begin their subscription and launch their future!

The subscription service is offered on a monthly or yearly basis as an individual, team, organization, educational institution or school district. Subscriptions can be cancelled at any time based on the refund policy (see website for details).

Please feel free to contact us for more information regarding bulk family, team, or organizational subscription membership purchases. Please ask us about the perks of strategic partnerships and alliances between our organization and yours.

How do I become a SMART JOCKS VIP Client?

You may make an appointment through Calendy on the website to seek personal coaching for domestic or international students regarding recruitment and training, college and career readiness, academic support, or current or future career advising.

Please email us at info@smartjocks.com to discuss speaking engagements, workshops (virtual or in person), or to book sports management and marketing consulting services.

SMART JOCKS

Workbook and Planner

The "SMART JOCKS Workbook and Planner" serves as a dream-catcher journal while reading along with the Amazon Best-Selling book "SMART JOCKS: 10 Lessons on Our Journey to Raise #1 Draft Picks On and Off the Court".

The workbook and planner also function as a calendar organizer to keep track of all your significant academic and athletic schedule responsibilities. Conquer procrastination and disorganization by logging important tasks like homework, research papers, tests, quizzes, group projects, services hours, game schedules, practice times, nutrition and fitness sessions, camps and showcase schedules, team huddles, family meetings, training video webinars and more!

Plan out your to do list for important logistics such as hotels, meals, transportation, and equipment inventory and maintenance for your academic and athletic travel calendar. Get reminders for critical deadlines to shake the habit of procrastination and crush your grades and your goals.

Be on top of your game with the

SMART JOCKS App and SMART JOCKS Workbook and Planner!

The Workbook & Planner Amazon Release Date is 8/8/18.
Reserve your autographed copies of the book and workbook and planner via the website today. Please email info@smartjocks.com for quotes for bulk purchases.

NOTES

SMART JOCKS

S

Thank You!

Thank you from the bottom of our hearts for purchasing and reading our book, "SMART JOCKS: 10 Lessons Along Our Journey to Raise #1 Draft Picks On and Off the Court". We hope you enjoyed it. If you have done so already, thank you for visiting the **www.smartjocks.com** website and registering for the **SMART JOCKS Tool Kit** which includes resources like the **SMART JOCKS Book and Workbook and Planner Bundle**, subscription to the **SMART JOCKS College & Career Readiness Portal** and access to the social media communities and webinar trainings that provide valuable innovative and motivational tools to become more knowledgeable and successful in life!

Adults - we hope you have learned some new tips to assist your child, mentee, player, team, and students along the journey to becoming #1 draft picks on and off the court. Students - we pray we have added some value to your life by helping you find clarity and making the bumps along the road a little bit smoother on your journey toward greatness.

This is our first book, and we would love your feedback because it will help us get better! Let's be social and stay connected so we can keep you updated on our activities. We are eager to help you in any way that we can. Please feel free to contact us for more information regarding bulk book/workbook & planner purchases, the SJ Portal membership or App subscriptions, speaking engagements, special events, or to schedule a one-on-one consultation.

SMART JOCKS - WE KEEP OUR EYE ON THE GOAL.

NOTES

SMART JOCKS

Let's Be Social!

To join the **SMART JOCKS Community** and help us advance our mission, sign up for a SMART JOCKS Tool Kit and Membership Subscription to the SJ Portal and follow us on social media. Tag us using the hashtags below and be eligible to win cool prizes & perks!

Website:	www.smartjocks.com
Facebook:	Smart Jocks
YouTube/Vimeo:	Smart Jocks
Twitter:	@smart_jocks
Periscope:	@smart_jocks
Snapchat:	@smart_jocks
Instagram:	@smart_jocks
Hashtags:	#SmartJock
	#SmartJocks
	#SmartJocksBook
	#SmartJocksMVP
	#SmartJocksPortal
	#SmartJocksToolKit
	#SmartJocksBookClub
	#SmartJocksAmbassador
	#SmartJocksInternational
	#SmartJocksHealthandFitness
	#SmartJocksWorkbookPlanner

Contact Us:
SMART JOCKS, LLC
P.O. Box 9635
Erie, PA 16505
(814) 732-0894
info@smartjocks.com